SHERWOOD ANDERSON

An American Career

John E. Bassett

SUP

Selinsgrove: Susquehanna University Press

©2006 by Rosemont Publishing & Printing Corp.

Associated University Presses
2010 Eastpark Boulevard
Cranbury, NJ 08512

The paper used in this publication meets the requirements of the American National Standard for Permanence of Paper for Printed Library Materials Z39.48–1984.

Library of Congress Cataloging-in-Publication Data

Bassett, John Earl, 1942-
   Sherwood Anderson : an American career / John E. Bassett.
     p. cm.
   Includes bibliographical references and index.
   ISBN 1-57591-102-7 (alk. paper)
1. Anderson, Sherwood, 1876-1941—Criticism and interpretation. I. Title.

PS3501.N4Z5484 2006
813'.52—dc22

                      2005015407

THIRD PRINTING 2007
PRINTED IN THE UNITED STATES OF AMERICA

For Kay

Contents

Preface

IT HAS BEEN MORE THAN A QUARTER CENTURY SINCE A CONCISE introduction to the career of Sherwood Anderson has appeared. Those by Irving Howe, Welford Taylor, and David Anderson have all been quite useful, and Rex Burbank's 1964 study of Anderson for Twayne Publishers was one of the most insightful and useful volumes in the American Writers Series. Between 1964 and now, to be sure, the entire profession of literary study has been turned upside down, and there is no way for a scholar of this generation not to feel influenced by and—whatever his or her own intellectual and political perspectives—at times enlightened by poststructuralism, New Historicism, and feminist theory among other theoretical discourses. Similarly an earlier generation was shaped by New Criticism, rigorous historical scholarship, and psychoanalytical thought. This essay, while a product of its own age, therefore raising issues and adopting perspectives less common to the earlier studies, is, like them, written for a broad range of Anderson readers.

The context for discussing racial- and gender-based patterns in fiction has changed, and while race- and gender-focused criticism will find far less of interest in Anderson than in, let us say, Faulkner, Anderson's swings between condescending bafflement and sympathetic engagement in developing female characters, as well as his patronizing racial motifs in *Dark Laughter* and elsewhere signify differently for today's readers than for readers a half century ago. Critics today are also more likely to see unresolved tensions in Anderson's work, such as that between a surface sympathy for displaced workers and baffled youths on the one hand and an inability to understand the connections between the anomie of his communities and an aggressive class-

9

based capitalism on the other, as being connected to the circumstances within which Anderson adopted a literary career out of his alienation from and even collapse during his career in business.

I do see Anderson as developing deliberately an American, and specifically a midwestern, literary career. American writers, and especially those born in the 1800s and early 1900s, have been self-conscious about the "American" aspect of their writing and at times equally about their region.[1] Anderson both implicitly and explicitly saw himself as a midwestern American artist unlike both Europeans, with longer established artistic traditions, and easterners, who, despite his periodic attraction to New York, he saw as lacking the rude vigor and vitality of the West. He identified with a country moving forward yet always nostalgically regretted what that progress entailed—industrialization, standardization, conformity. He sought sources for a renewed vitality, but the romantic images—the Negro, the Female, (less so) the Mountaineer—remained abstract whereas the victims of modernization were portrayed vividly and movingly.

Anderson was always best at the image, the impression, the sketch, the tale, the essay, not the integrated longer work. He captured feelings and impressions, not changes in characters or communities over time and not complex social and economic issues. What he did well few have done better, and his best work retains a significant place in the canon of modern American writing. It continues to move and enlighten the sensitive reader. Today people are adjusting to another period of enormous change, one marked by psychological and ethical and social adjustments due to, for example, unprecedented biomedical advances, a communication revolution, waves of immigration and demographic shifts, and renewed tribalism and terrorism. At such a time Anderson's poignant and even startling impressions of the lonely soul, the displaced worker, the fanatic, and the questor may well take on new meanings and significance for another generation.

Anderson, however, has not recently been as widely read and studied as he once was. In my research I had an experience similar to the one I had not long ago undertaking a project on Thomas Wolfe. The 1950s, 1960s, and 1970s were very active decades in Anderson (and Wolfe) scholarship and criticism. In the two and a half decades since 1980, however, outside of edited and collected writings, research guides, and biographies, few critical books have appeared on Anderson; few articles in the top-tier literary journals are on Anderson; and the summary of Anderson commentary in the annual *American Literary Scholarship* can generally be handled in one paragraph. The *Winesburg Eagle*, now the *Sherwood Anderson Review*, has continued to publish items of significance to Anderson specialists; and certainly Anderson has benefited from the intelligent attention he has received from such dedicated scholars as Walter Rideout, William Sutton, Ray Lewis White, Hilbert Campbell, and David D. Anderson. Nonetheless it is harder to find his works seriously discussed in the general discourse about modern American literature, outside of studies of the short-story composite, which almost necessarily must cover *Winesburg, Ohio*.

There is no collected American edition of Anderson's works, but there should be. There is a collected twenty-one-volume edition published in Japan by Rinsen Book Company. Ray Lewis White edited three volumes—*A Story-Teller's Story*, *Tar*, and *Marching Men*—in a critical edition begun by Case Western Reserve University Press between 1968 and 1972. The project received mixed reviews from textual scholars and was never carried further. White has more recently published a useful critical edition of *Winesburg, Ohio*.[2] Students of Anderson do benefit, moreover, from a number of published volumes of Anderson's letters and diaries and previously uncollected writings as well as bibliographical aids. There is also a substantial body of unpublished drafts of incomplete novels and stories, no buried masterpieces to be sure, but a wealth of material that for the Anderson scholar and student can provide significant additional perspectives on Anderson's development as a writer. Some of these texts, most notably "Mary Cochran," "Talbott Whittingham," "Father Abraham," and "Ohio Pagans" are covered here because they do cast helpful light on Anderson's published books and stories.

I am particularly grateful to Diana Haskell and her staff at the Newberry Library for assisting me in using its extensive Sherwood Anderson collections. Short quotations from unpublished materials in the collections are used with permission of the Newberry Library. I am also grateful to William Sutton for a conversation early on in the project, to Joseph Flora for suggesting the project, to the staffs of the libraries of Case Western Reserve University and Clark University for countless favors, and to Shirley Granlund for helping me prepare the typescript.

Chronology

1876	Sherwood Anderson born September 13 in Camden, Ohio, the third of six children born to Irwin Anderson and Emma Smith Anderson.
1883	Anderson family settles in Clyde, Ohio.
1895	Emma Smith Anderson dies.
1896	Anderson moves to Chicago, works in warehouses.
1898	Enters military service, spends a short period in Cuba in Spanish-American War.
1899	Enrolls in Wittenberg Academy, spends one year in residence.
1900	Returns to Chicago and positions as advertising writer and salesman.
1904	Marries Cornelia Lane on May 16 (divorced 1916).
1906	Moves to Cleveland as president of United Factories Co.
1907	Moves to Elyria and starts a series of business ventures; son Robert is born. During next few years begins writing fiction, including his early novels.
1912	Has a breakdown.
1913	Returns to Chicago, separates from Cornelia, rejoins Taylor-Critchfield Agency, becomes part of Chicago Renaissance group of writers.
1914	First short story, "The Rabbit-Pen," published in *Harper's* in June.
1915	Begins writing tales that become *Winesburg, Ohio*.
1916	*Windy McPherson's Son;* marries Tennessee Mitchell (divorced 1924).
1917	*Marching Men;* begins to spend time in New York with Van Wyck Brooks, Waldo Frank, and the *Seven Arts* crowd.

1918	*Mid-American Chants.*
1919	*Winesburg, Ohio.*
1920	*Poor White.*
1921	*The Triumph of the Egg;* wins first *Dial* award; travels to Europe and meets James Joyce, Gertrude Stein, and other writers.
1922	Spends the first of several periods in New Orleans.
1923	*Many Marriages; Horses and Men.*
1924	*A Story-Teller's Story;* marries Elizabeth Prall (divorced 1932) after a year in residence in Reno to gain divorce from Tennessee Mitchell.
1925	*Dark Laughter.*
1926	*Tar: A Midwest Childhood; Sherwood Anderson's Notebook;* goes on a lecture tour.
1927	*A New Testament;* trip to Europe; buys farm near Marion, Virginia, and two local newspapers; goes on another lecture tour.
1929	*Hello Towns!*
1930	Travels with Eleanor Copenhaver to mill towns and becomes more involved with workers.
1931	*Perhaps Women.*
1932	*Beyond Desire.*
1933	*Death in the Woods and Other Stories;* marries Eleanor Copenhaver.
1934	*No Swank;* staging of *Winesburg, Ohio* by Hedgerow Theater.
1935	*Puzzled America.*
1936	*Kit Brandon.*
1937	National Institute of Arts and Letters elects Anderson to membership; *Plays: Winesburg and Others.*
1940	*Home Town.*
1941	Dies March 8, en route to South America.
1942	*Sherwood Anderson's Memoirs*, edited by Paul Rosenfeld.

SHERWOOD ANDERSON

1

An Ohio Pagan

INTRODUCTION

LIKE THOMAS WOLFE AND JOHN DOS PASSOS, SHERWOOD ANDERSON has been disappearing from literary histories of America. Like Sinclair Lewis, Carl Sandburg, Edgar Lee Masters, and other stars of the Chicago Renaissance but for Theodore Dreiser, he seems to be disappearing from college syllabi, although *Winesburg, Ohio* does occasionally show up. Because of that book, a number of strong stories, and a good bit of underrated nonfiction, however, Anderson should and will maintain a visible minor presence for some time to come. He also remains of interest for living one of those uniquely American careers, a mixture of naïve romantic artist and somewhat disingenuous self-created myth.

For a brief period, 1920 to 1923 more or less, Anderson had a great deal of critical prestige. He had started his literary career, as distinguished from his years of writing blurbs, sketches, and short items for advertising magazines, only a few years earlier when in his mid-thirties. After 1923, his reputation declined, although some of the best work still lay ahead. Anderson's final fifteen years, while prolific, were marked by parallel attempts to do something new and to recapture a genius and initiative he once had. Although he published two novels and several stories in those years, his primary output was nonfictional.

The story begins back in 1876. Anderson was born in the same decade as Frank Norris, Stephen Crane, and Dreiser, all of whose first novels had appeared by the end of 1900 and two of whom were dead, as was Harold Frederic, by 1902. Partly because of his late start,

Anderson is often grouped, however, with the much younger William Faulkner, Ernest Hemingway, and F. Scott Fitzgerald as a postwar writer; and it is true that, as they were for the Lost Generation, those older writers were for Anderson part of the given, part of the tradition within which and against which he wrote. Unlike that next generation, however, he was not shaped by the Great War or the intellectual fervor of the postwar years, although Gertrude Stein had a significant influence on him. Rather, the post–Civil War forces of business expansion, frontier closings, and growth of cities would have affected Anderson as they did the writers of the 1890s and early 1900s. Like Dreiser, he grew up in small midwestern towns and in a somewhat dysfunctional family with several siblings, and in his late teens he went off to the big city. Unlike Dreiser he was able more as an insider to move into the world of business and country-club life, although he turned away from that life and from his loyal wife Cornelia. Crane, too, rejected his "establishment" opportunities but lived a faster, shorter, more adventurous, and outrageous life. Like Edgar Allan Poe, Nathanael West, Hart Crane, and Wolfe he was one of the romantic, lived-fast, wrote-well, died-young American artists. Unlike Stephen Crane, Norris (whose formal education separates him from his contemporaries), Frederic, and Dreiser, Anderson did not come to fiction through newspaper journalism. Rather advertising gave him his preliterary training, and also gave him a way of life to repudiate.

BIOGRAPHY

Anderson was born in Camden, Ohio, on September 13, 1876, eleven and a half years after the Civil War ended and shortly before the election of Rutherford B. Hayes would spell the end of Radical Reconstruction. By 1879 the Anderson family had moved from Camden, near the southwest corner of the state, to Caledonia near Marion in central Ohio, and then by 1883 to Clyde, in the north between Cleveland and Toledo and not far from Thomas Edison's home town of Milan. Anderson stayed in Clyde until moving to Chicago.[1]

Irwin Anderson was a harness maker who had served in the war, but who in Sherwood's childhood lost his business, suffered a streak of bad luck, took a series of odd jobs including house painting, and more and more came to be seen as a failure, a weak man, a ne'er-do-

well. Anderson's early fiction and the memoirs reveal a hostility the
son felt toward his father, but gradually that is tempered and subsequent writings indicated an appreciation of the father's vitality and
at least a vicarious resolution of the relationship for Sherwood.[2] Irwin was the storyteller, the role Anderson converted into a career.
When, however, his mother died in 1895 and Irwin soon thereafter
left town, Sherwood retained little if any positive feeling toward his
father.

Emma Smith Anderson raised the children. A strong, silent, religious woman, she kept the family together through the moves and
Irwin's lapses, but died when only forty-two. Sherwood felt some
shame at having his mother take in laundry and make other de-
meaning adjustments due to the family's genteel poverty. There
were six children overall, five boys and a sister, Stella, who left college in order to make a living and later became a quite pious Christian. She died in her thirties. Except for Emma's mother, a difficult
woman who was finally asked to leave the house, few if any roles were
played in Sherwood's life by any larger family of aunts, uncles, or
cousins. Like many a small-town lad in those postwar years, Anderson never finished high school, though he developed a love for
books and theater. Romances such as those by James Fenimore
Cooper were his favorites. Out of both necessity and ambition, he
left school to hawk newspapers, do yard jobs, work in a bicycle factory, and tend horses in a livery stable. Horses remained a favorite
source of fantasy for him. During those years he also received the
suitable nickname "Jobby."

If Ohio was Anderson's childhood home and Virginia the home
of his final years, Chicago was the center of most of his adult life, although he did not live there continuously for a long period. Anderson's first years in Chicago came when, Emma having passed away
and Irwin having deserted, he—like George Willard, one might
say—left his home village in 1895 for the city. During his first two
years there, he found work mostly in warehouses. He lived with and
was close to an old Clyde friend, Clifton Paden, who later, under the
name John Emerson, became a film producer and remained close to
and supportive of Anderson. His first stretch in Chicago, between
then and 1906, was interrupted by military service in the Spanish-
American War, including a stint in Cuba in 1899, and a year spent at
Wittenberg Academy in Springfield, Ohio, a positive experience in-

tellectually but not one he sought to continue. Trillena White, a teacher at Wittenberg, provided a positive and continuing influence he always appreciated.[3]

Returning to Chicago in 1900, Anderson found work through a series of connections, first with a publisher and then in advertising with the White Agency, later Long-Critchfield. Despite a limited formal education but doubtless in part because of being an avid reader, Anderson showed a skill in copy writing and in sketches, blurbs, and epigrams for trade journals including *Agricultural Advisor*. He continued to read—authors such as George Borrow, Thomas Carlyle, and Robert Louis Stevenson—but at least on the surface was also committed to succeeding in his new business career. In a letter to Floyd Dell in 1920 he said, "I was in business for a long time and the truth is I was a smooth son of a bitch."[4]

In 1904 Anderson married Cornelia Lane, a young Toledo woman who had graduated from the College for Women at Western Reserve University. The first of four wives, Cornelia was the only one to bear him children—Robert (born 1907), John (1908), and Marion (1911), known as Mimi. In 1906 Anderson and Cornelia moved to Cleveland, where he briefly and unsuccessfully managed a mail-order business, United Factories. In September 1907 the family settled in Elyria, where Anderson ran a paint firm and other companies until having a personal crisis and nervous breakdown in 1912. That collapse, which took place on the streets of Cleveland, has never been fully understood but does define a major turning point in Anderson's life. From all signs he had come to feel estranged from and restless within the established family-business-society framework of his Elyria routine. His early writings include several patterns of confinement, flight, and self-destructive tendencies. He had been at least superficially successful, but as he lost interest in his career he was also smoking and drinking heavily, getting moody and erratic in his behavior, and spending more and more time alone in an upstairs room writing fiction, including very likely parts of what became his first two published novels.

After the collapse in November 1912, Anderson returned to Chicago and a job with the Taylor-Critchfield Agency. Although the family tried to reestablish itself by means of a retreat to the Ozark Mountains in 1913, for all intents and purposes the return to Chicago marked a permanent separation from Cornelia, who later began a career as a school teacher in Indiana. Anderson meanwhile combined his advertising work with a commitment to a literary career. In his first year back in Chicago he benefited from contact with a group that included Floyd Dell, Ben Hecht, Margery Curry, and other writers. *Harper's* accepted what became his first published short story, "The Rabbit Pen" (1914). He worked on other novels, "Mary Cochran" and "Talbott Whittingham" and one called "Immaturity," that were not published except in parts as stories but contributed to his growth as a writer. He frequented literary and artistic gatherings, took part in a group called the Dill Pickle Club, tried painting, and came across the prose of Gertrude Stein. Sophisticated doyen of modernism, she was perhaps an unlikely inspiration for a romantic provincial; but her prose, such as that in *Tender Buttons*, as much as any other influence provided a key to unlock Anderson's real strength at the impressionistic sketch. Later Stein and Anderson became friends and correspondents.

In 1916 and 1917 Anderson's first two novels, *Windy McPherson's Son* and *Marching Men*, were published by John Lane Co. with some help from Dell and Dreiser and to more good reviews, including one by Hecht, than they probably deserved. A collection of verse, *Mid-American Chants*, written mostly in 1914 and 1915, imitative of Whitman and compared with Sandburg's poems, appeared in 1918. As David Anderson says, it may be most important for indicating Anderson's assertion of a self-consciously midwestern voice.[5] Meanwhile, in 1916 Anderson remarried; early in 1917 he moved to New York; and between November 1915 and 1917 he was writing the sketches that would make up *Winesburg, Ohio*. His new wife was Tennessee Mitchell. An attractive, independent, liberated "new woman" three years older than Anderson, Tennessee, who was originally from Jackson, Michigan, had a background in music and dance. In 1916 they were fellow strugglers in the world of art enjoying literary and artistic circles, but during their marriage they actually maintained separate homes in Chicago. They were divorced in 1924, though the marriage had been falling apart for several years. Anderson spent an entire year in Reno arranging for the final divorce.

The move to New York in 1917 was temporary as Chicago remained Anderson's base. He never particularly loved Chicago, but it was the urban center of the region, the Midwest, with which he most closely identified. For the next few years he alternated time in

Chicago with time in Alabama, Wisconsin, Europe, New Orleans, and frequently New York. New York brought him into regular contact with a new set of friends and influences. Among these were the *Seven Arts* crowd that included Waldo Frank and Van Wyck Brooks with their radical challenge to traditionalism and literary convention, but also Paul Rosenfeld, who for the rest of Anderson's life remained especially close, as well as Anita Loos and her husband, his old friend John Emerson, and in 1922 Alfred Stieglitz. His first trip to Europe, in 1921 with Rosenfeld, opened him up to a whole new world and gave him an opportunity to meet James Joyce and other writers, including Stein and her circle.[6]

Creation of the Winesburg stories began with "The Book of the Grotesque" and "Hands" in 1915 and continued incrementally for two years. They represented a significant shift in Anderson's style toward impressionistic sketches, in this case connected by location, mood, and theme. Influences were numerous—the prose of Stein, Anderson's working through of his artistic persona in "Talbott Whittingham," earlier sketch writers like Borrow, the cast of people he had met in Chicago and Clyde, his own reflection on aesthetic issues as conveyed in an intriguing 1915 essay "The New Note," and doubtless much more. Ben Huebsch published *Winesburg, Ohio* in May 1919, by which time Anderson was back in Chicago. Many reviews, including those by H. L. Mencken, a young Hart Crane, and Burton Rascoe, were quite positive.

While in New York in 1918, however, Anderson returned to the extended narrative and drafted *Poor White*, published in 1920. It shows him ambitious to move beyond short impressionistic sketches out to a larger social panorama of a midwestern town being changed by capital-based commerce and industry. He began with the same format he had used before, a restless youth leaving his village for a new and more promising place, but gradually became more interested in social changes in the town itself and so focused on other characters. While marred by structural problems, the book remains a kind of companion work to *Winesburg, Ohio*, the only full-length fiction exploring a town rather than an individual or pair of individuals. *Poor White* is to some Anderson scholars Anderson's best novel, but it sold poorly and it received mixed reviews.

After completing *Winesburg, Ohio* and while writing *Poor White* and later *Many Marriages*, Anderson also wrote short stories, including many of his best tales. They were published in two splendid collections, *The Triumph of the Egg* (1921) and *Horses and Men* (1923). Both received excellent reviews from critics such as Mencken, John Peale Bishop, Newton Arvin, and William Rose Benét. The combination of *Winesburg, Ohio, Poor White*, and these collections elevated Anderson to his highest level of public and critical prestige from about 1920 to 1923.

At the same time his correspondence and writings would seem to suggest some continuing uncertainty about his own artistry. He had adopted in his New York phase a more sophisticated or at least pseudo-sophisticated front, and a few tales depend on an ironic voice with which he was never comfortable. At the same time he liked to present himself as a crude but virile midwesterner unlike the sophisticated effete New Yorkers he had met. His second marriage began to unravel, and Anderson entered a phase that included two novels revolving around unhappy marriages and stories of confused gender relations. By 1922, moreover, he was in love again, and in 1924 he married Elizabeth Prall, a midwestern lady he met in New York but whose academic parents then lived in Berkeley, California.

In the early 1920s Anderson failed to finish at least two books, "Ohio Pagans" and a manuscript on Abraham Lincoln, "Father Abraham."[7] He did complete *Many Marriages* (1923), a bizarre romance of a midlife crisis, and then *Dark Laughter* (1925), his best-selling book. He published *A Story-Teller's Story* (1924), an engaging and imaginative autobiography of Anderson as "American artist," and then a bit later *Tar* (1926), a short autobiographical fiction. He also came out with a second collection of verse, *A New Testament* (1927), and *Sherwood Anderson's Notebook* (1926), a potpourri, at times quite well written, of autobiography, criticism, and essays. During this period Anderson came to know other writers, including Dreiser, Fitzgerald, and Hamilton Basso, as well as Faulkner and Hemingway, both of whom always showed a certain condescension toward him, Hemingway, for example, rather cruelly in *Torrents of Spring* and Faulkner more gently in *Mosquitoes*.

The last fourteen years of his life Anderson lived in the Blue Ridge area of Virginia, building a home in Troutdale and purchasing two newspapers in nearby Marion. His brothers and son Robert moved or visited there. He originally settled there with Elizabeth, but by 1928 their marriage was falling apart. The divorce did not take place until 1932, but by 1928 he had met and by 1930 had fallen in love with a much younger woman, Eleanor Copenhaver. Son Bob managed the newspapers and Anderson traveled around a great deal. He loved the Blue Ridge, but as in New York he self-consciously felt an outsider. Eleanor raised his political consciousness and took him to mill towns, at times as in Danville the site of a major strike, where he listened sympathetically to the lives and tales of factory workers. Although in a sense always the Emersonian individualist and never a consistent enough leftist to satisfy any variety of communist or socialist, Anderson signed manifestos, engaged in protests, gave political talks, and wrote sympathetic portrayals of working-class figures.

His dominant mode of writing became the short nonfiction work, items put together in diverse collections between 1929 and 1935. *Hello Towns* (1929) consists of pieces of mountain journalism, essays, and sketches, some using a created vernacular character named Buck Fever. *Perhaps Women* (1932) is a set of essays on the failure of the American male and the potential of women to redefine a new vitality. *No Swank* (1934) is a collection of diverse essays, and *Puzzled America* (1935) has essays and sketches about the South and the Midwest during the Depression.

Anderson and Eleanor married in 1933, and from all available evidence his final eight years were happy ones personally. He also returned to fiction in the 1930s for two novels and a collection of stories, *Death in the Woods and Other Stories* (1933). In that book the title story, whose earlier versions had been drafted years before, and "Brother Death" are excellent, some of the others disappointing. *Beyond Desire* (1932) is Anderson's one attempt at a political novel, such as it is, revolving in part around a strike like one in Gastonia in 1929. *Kit Brandon* (1936) is an at times fascinating novel about an engaging mountain woman, a driver for bootleggers, told through the eyes of an amazed Andersonian middle-aged narrator, trying, like Nick Carraway with Jay Gatsby, to bring sense and meaning to the story he has learned.

Anderson wrote a few other tales and sketches, published a collection of four plays including a stage version of *Winesburg, Ohio,* and crafted an extended essay called *Home Town,* which Kim Townsend discusses as an elegy for the American small town.[8] His major efforts in the final years went toward completing his *Memoirs,* which were never finished but were edited and published posthumously by Paul Rosenfeld in 1942 and then edited in a more authoritative version by Ray Lewis White in 1969. Not surprisingly the book is delightful for its sketches of dozens of people Anderson knew, not for any thematic or conceptual wholeness. He continued until the end of his life to interact with writers, to seek new experiences, to make sense of what he and America were all about. On March 8, 1941, he died from complications after swallowing a toothpick while onboard ship with Eleanor as they were sailing to South America, a new place for him.

Born a decade after the Civil War, Anderson died as war raged in Europe but did not yet include soldiers from the United States. He lived through the transformation of America from an agricultural to an industrial economy, and he always explored the loneliness and confusion that individuals face in navigating the passages of their life from adolescence to adulthood to old age, as well as the passages of their community, at times toward a more depersonalized, mechanical commodification of the self. Anderson, the brash and confident village youth, became the initially successful but frustrated and confused city businessman, then the questor for an alternative life as a writer, gradually maturing within that role if never beyond self-consciousness about his background. By the end he was a more avuncular observer of and commenter on the American scene. He wrote a limited amount of excellent work, but what is excellent retains its resonance for today's reader, and the story of Anderson the writer itself continues to have a poignancy for Americans, perhaps because they continue to be puzzled by and concerned with what is peculiarly American about writing in the United States and how the modern self adjusts its Emersonian and Jeffersonian myths to a reality where they may seem less and less convincing. No two lives of American writers are the same; but one finds similarities in the regional self-consciousness of westerners like Twain, Howells, Dreiser, and Anderson, who are also more assertively "American" about their work than are writers such as James, Henry Adams, and Frederic whose roots are northeastern.

2

A New Profession

WINDY MCPHERSON'S SON AND *MARCHING MEN* ARE APPRENTICE NOVELS, of interest to the Anderson scholar but, perhaps like *Soldiers' Pay* and *Mosquitoes* among Faulkner's works, of less interest to other readers. *Soldiers' Pay* and *Mosquitoes*, to be sure, were followed by many wonderful novels, whereas Anderson never wrote any truly first-rate novels and in fact wrote his best book only a few years later, really as *Windy McPherson's Son* and *Marching Men* were being published. *Winesburg, Ohio*, however, was a new start in a fresh form, and from then on Anderson's best work was generally in short forms.

Nonetheless the two apprentice novels do reveal the seeds of fictional themes and patterns that continue in later works. The young man, frustrated, seeking to fulfill his vision, fuzzy though it may be, is replaced later by the somewhat older man seeking a happier primitivism as an alternative to his life style, and he is then replaced by the observer-narrator watching, learning from, appreciating new centers of vitality. But there is always the frustrated, ingenuous figure, at first from the provinces heading off to the big city or wider world and later from the city returning to a "healthier" primitive world.

Actually, Anderson's literary apprenticeship should be reviewed through a book of poems and four novels, two published and two not published, "Mary Cochran" and "Talbott Whittingham." In each of the four prose manuscripts Anderson projects versions of himself through his protagonists, Sam McPherson and Talbott Whittingham, more directly, and Beaut McGregor and Mary Cochran quite indirectly. Sam is the ambitious young Horatio Alger figure on the road to success, Talbott at times but not consistently his portrait of the artist, Beaut the talented "one of the roughs" angry and frustrated that the world will not line up as it should, Mary the innocent who dreams of romantic parentage and true love but finds the mundane compromises of Chicago about as good as it gets. Only when Anderson stopped developing dominant protagonists at the center of his fictions, when he turned to the impressionistic sketches and short tales of *Winesburg, Ohio*, with a recessed protagonist-observer, did he write from his strengths. They were never those of systematic psychological insight or panoramic social tapestries. In his final novel in the 1930s he returned again to the observer-listener, and in some of his best tales his strengths show up through the impressions and observations of an at times baffled observer more than through direct portrayal of characters.

One motif common to all of Anderson's early novels is the young person leaving his village, usually midwestern, and going toward or to a city or larger town, often Chicago. The motif is an old one, though almost always ambiguous, suggesting both the promise of fulfilling ambition and the corruption of a fallen world, both flight from parochialism and the loss of wholeness. In American fiction it appears in works as early as *Arthur Mervyn* and as close to Anderson's period as Dreiser's *Sister Carrie* and Frederic's *The Damnation of Theron Ware*. For Anderson it was autobiographical but also, at least until the 1920s, emblematic of his own continuing need to flee, to run away from or toward something—family, marriage, business, constraints, himself. In the last part of his life the pattern was reversed, the city itself no longer a meaningful symbol of a goal, although from the very beginning Anderson had treated the city ironically. It was never a satisfactory goal. None of the characters who go there find what they are seeking. George Willard's story stops before he gets there, and the frustrations and grotesque traits of Winesburg's inhabitants, as much as in this book they are intertwined with the landscape of a repressive village, were drawn from Anderson's observations in Chicago as well as from what he had seen in Clyde, Ohio.

Windy McPherson's Son (1916) is the story of Sam McPherson, son of a small-town house painter, a boastful failure. Sam, an enterprising newsboy, learns that making money is the key to success and identity and becomes a buyer for a local company. His mother having died, Sam, feeling hatred for his self-pitying drunkard of a father, then goes on the road as a traveling buyer and ends up in Chicago as a trusted associate of Colonel Tom Rainey, chief executive of a firearms company. Gradually taking over the firm, Sam also marries Rainey's daughter. Their marriage is fraught with problems—the death of each newborn child, Sue's shift of commitment from having perfect children to social reform, and Sam's obsession with financial success. When he betrays Sue's trust, at the height of his economic power and the nadir of his moral behavior, Sam flees "on a quest of truth." The rest of the novel consists of the "vagabond's" wanderings for several years from town to town and state to state, helping factory women on strike, listening to all sorts of people, dissipating, and yearning at times for the alleged power and understanding of an artist. The story ends in a rather incredible sequence of Sam, having assumed in St. Louis the guardianship of three children of a drunken woman, delivering the children to Sue and thereby, we are led to believe, satisfying her "mother hunger." Like Hawthorne's Wakefield, Sam is welcomed back into his house, having learned he "cannot run away from life" but must "face it."

The strength of *Windy McPherson's Son* lies mostly in the first section, the story of Sam's family problems and Horatio Alger–like success. The rest of the book has less conceptual coherence, although Anderson's point is that success in the business world may be unsatisfying and perhaps even morally debilitating. If the first part of the novel is autobiographically suggestive, the rest may be revelatory of Anderson's fantasies.

Sam McPherson is the most successfully drawn of the four early protagonists, although by the middle of the manuscript Anderson is uncertain what to do with him next. The young Sam, however, is an engaging and convincing adolescent, sensitive to the problems in his family, vulnerable to a series of influences, ambitious but unsure from step to step what that really means. In this book Anderson works through his antagonism toward his father, a man he remembered as a failure, an ineffectual parent if occasionally charming raconteur, who deserted his family after his wife's death. As has often been shown, Irwin Anderson actually had an honorable Civil War record and a successful business as a harness maker until it failed when Sherwood was young. That was not, however, the father he knew, and the resentment Anderson felt comes through in several works, most fully in *Windy McPherson's Son*, even in the title. Windy is a drunken, boastful, blustering old fool. His failures now make him the butt of community laughter, inspiring Sam to swear, "You may laugh at that fool Windy, but you shall never laugh at Sam McPherson" (33).[1]

Sam's alternative family is Joe Wildman's, but his alternative and finally unsatisfactory father is John Telfer. Telfer, a misogynist, dandy, and town orator, is also a failure, but his verbal skills and poise make him appear a success. As a "man of leisure" not a failure, he is the envy of working people, one chosen to chair town meetings, a man who impresses Sam with his love of books and respect for the "sacredness" of art. Gradually Sam realizes Telfer is one from whom he can learn, as Prince Hal does from Falstaff, but not one he should emulate. Gradually Telfer's cynicism comes through, his belief not only that making money (he has not) is the key to the good life but also that cheating and lying are appropriate American tactics for making it. Ironically moneymaking becomes like art in his value system, in effect a substitute for art, despite art's "sacredness," not the opposite of art. The poor artist in his garret has freedom for neither art nor what money can buy.

Telfer's cynicism extends to women, the root of all men's problems, diabolically clever and apt to "retard" a boy's growth, like cigarettes one infers. He blames women for his own failure to be more than "a village cut-up" (71). Under the sway of Telfer's notions, Sam denies his devoted teacher Mary Underwood. While he later atones and becomes her loyal proponent, he never fully sorts out his feelings for her, making bizarre marriage proposals as he also seeks in her a second mother. Mary is one of those intriguing minor Anderson figures, a pale, tired, graying, reticent, intelligent, affectionate teacher with a hint of mild scandal about her reputation and an implication of rich potential frustrated by a narrow-minded community.

To Telfer sex not art is the opposite of moneymaking, and much of Sam's confusion derives from his problems dealing with women. Book I, in fact, has near the end a curious essay on "woman," marked by an image of women who live hollow lives, have rigid ideas and little compassion, not like Mary but like the women who slander her and deny her humanity. She is the alternative mother to Telfer's alternative father, but again an unfulfilled person.

Women and sexuality continue as major themes in Anderson's fiction, generally more revealing of unresolved personal tensions than of significant insights. It might seem at first that most of Anderson's early women are passive, pathetic, and ill, but Anderson's males can be just as passive or pathetic, and he also drew a number of strong if not always clearly directed women such as Margaret Ormsby, Clara Butterworth, and Mary Cochran. In *Windy McPherson's Son*, following Jane McPherson, Mary Underwood, and Janet Eberly, moreover, Sue Rainey enters the story. After that point, to be sure, Anderson seems unsure how to continue the story of Sam, once he succeeds, or how to develop a strong woman like Sue that Sam can wed but not control. The novel at times gets rather silly. While Sue's obsession with having children who will be the fulfillment of her vision is credible, there are bizarre passages in the conversations between Sue and Sam. The two also reverse roles on their camping honeymoon: she instructs Sam in hunting and sex, and even that is credible given Sam's narrow dedication to moneymaking. There is a less credible shift in Sue's personality, with her failure to bear children who can survive, to the role of settlement-house reformer surrounded by "corsetless" feminists of "the movement" while Sam now lusts for children of his loins. What is credible is Sam's betrayal of Sue, his lie that he will protect Rainey's company during consolidation of the firearms industry. It is the high point of the arc of Sam's success and the mark of his moral decay. Sam's decline continues with new power, manipulations, stock raids, and a "sickness to the soul" until he flees his own rot, seeking his lost soul and "Truth" for the rest of the book.

Beyond Anderson's immature craft, however, there is a good bit of interest here for anyone studying Anderson's career. Whether he had read Dreiser's *The Financier* at this point or not, this is Anderson's version of the Frank Cowperwood story, the Horatio Alger character who works hard, becomes a capitalist success, and gets the woman of his choice but at the cost of his soul. Whereas Dreiser, however, has a conceptual grasp of his larger subject matter, of character and of the world of finance, to follow his themes through to a natural conclusion, Anderson is less confident once Sam gains control of the Rainey Company. In one sense Sister Carrie had been Dreiser's comparable autobiographical character—despite a change in gender, and, to be sure, had Dreiser not discovered Hurstwood in mid-text, it is not clear how he would have made the rest of a full novel revolve only around Carrie's personality and development.

Anderson spends more time than Dreiser detailing the problems of the hero's home life and hometown. Young Sam from the beginning is on the move, able to outsmart fellow newsboy Fatty as easily as Tom Sawyer outsmarts his chums, contemptuous of his blustering father, hungry awhile for religion, or any lodestar, but early on rejecting it because of the miserable representatives of religion that he sees in town, admiring at times the atheist blasphemer Mike Mc-Carthy or the dandy John Telfer, and determined to be a man of money, the one common denominator for respect, it would seem. Having served his apprenticeship under Freedom Smith, having watched his mother die, Sam is prepared to go out in the world, unconnected to his past but trained to be a "solid citizen" in the community of his choice.

Sam's work as a traveling buyer puts him on the road for the first time, anticipating his longer journey at the end of the story. Anderson uses the first trip as a means of setting up certain motifs—the cornfields as a positive image, business as a sport rewarding the ruthless fighter (but not unlike science and art in its promise of meaning and satisfaction), women as a force not to be understood, and against that the male bonding of a strange trip to Wisconsin with two friends. By the time Sam works for Colonel Rainey he has become the selfish financier lusting for control, satisfied only when he becomes a company leader. Then, Anderson ironically adds, Sam has become merely a type, a gang, but then, also, Anderson has to decide whether to follow his character through to the logical conclusion of what has taken place, as Dreiser does with Cowperwood, or to do something else. Although there may seem to be an autobiographical parallel between Sam's repudiation of his success and Anderson's flight from Elyria, there is little thematic or artistic coherence to Sam's wanderings in the final parts of the book.

Anderson revised the final chapter of *Windy McPherson's Son* for a new edition in 1922. The basic episode does not change; Sam and three children are welcomed back in Sue's house, now moved to a New England village from the house by the Hudson River in the 1916 version, both far from the Illinois of their first home. The revised chapter is more reflective, less straight narrative, and also indicates that now "Sam McPherson is a living American. He is a rich man."[2] Sam's ambivalence about domesticity gets more emphasis, and his final motivation seems to be the need to move beyond self to the other, to love, to understanding other lives.[3]

MARCHING MEN

Like *Windy McPherson's Son, Marching Men* tells the story of a youth from a small town who goes off to find his future in Chicago. The two books have much in common, but the youths and their goals are very different. Sam begins as the shrewd but naïve protagonist of a Horatio Alger story; Beaut McGregor, however, is defined by his rage, his hatreds, his contempt for others, as well as his red hair and large nose. *Windy McPherson's Son* carries Sam to success and dissatisfaction with success. Beaut has some minor victories, but it is never clear what "success" would even mean to him. This second novel also trails off at the end with only the fuzziest of suggestions about its meaning. Nonetheless, in May 1917 Anderson wrote to Babs Finley saying that "the whole big message of my life is bound into that volume."[4] Each of his early manuscripts works through one of his own dilemmas from a different perspective. Sam McPherson's story traces a pattern of business success followed by a moral awakening and flight from that life. If Beaut's story carries the "big message of my life," it is a message of a thirst for the kind of power to change his world and its people not literally in the way Beaut himself follows but through writing. The fantasy beneath the book is of the talented youth developing into a powerful influence on others. That power and fantasy are then portrayed through Talbott Whittingham, the artist in embryo, and more effectively through George Willard, who listens and watches and then goes off to the city and to accomplishments undefined.

Marching Men opens in Coal Creek, Pennsylvania. Norman "Beaut" McGregor is the son of a coal miner, who dies in a fire trying to be a hero, and a mother who runs a bakery. Unlike Sam's village, Coal Creek is an unredeemably hideous place, although the nearby valley, to be sure, is more idyllic. Beaut hates his home and gladly leaves it in 1893 for Chicago. Filled with contempt for mankind, he desires to be its master, although to what end is unclear. His usual wish is to organize people, to get them marching and in line and under control. Although he is critical of men for being disorganized and undirected and weak, he would if given control, it appears, make them more robotic and less human. Anderson scholars often read *Marching Men* as anticipating fascism and its militaristic impulse to organize men as armies. Fascism, however, did have a political agenda, whereas it is unclear what Beaut's agenda would be if he could organize workers of his world. In a most stimulating recent article, Mark Whalen argues that *Marching Men* reflects a deep-seated concern with manhood, masculinity, and "gender politics." Despite the book's lack of a real political argument, Whalen suggests, moreover, its "exaltation of the collective male military body" and the connections it draws between "military conquest, creativity, and phallic sexual gratification" are astonishingly protofascist, albeit tendencies made more problematic in *Winesburg, Ohio.*[5]

There is ambivalence in a reader's relationship to Beaut. He has enough of the romantic idealist to keep one's sympathy, and what he dislikes or disdains a reader will generally also dislike. The cruelty in his nature, his single-minded obsessions, and his belief in the "pitiful insignificance of the individual" (217), however, create ironic distance between him and both author and reader.[6] Frank Turner, a barber and maker of violins, has, like Anderson, split from his wife and now, "free" and contented with prostitutes, maintains a cynical contempt for women. The more romantic McGregor cannot accept that cynicism and finally repudiates Frank as Sam McPherson had John Telfer.

The plot as it unfolds in Chicago has two strands, one around Beaut and a set of women, particularly Edith Carson and Margaret Ormsby, the other around his "career" as he becomes an organizer of men. The former ends in uncertainty as Beaut is torn between two very different women and Margaret is torn between Beaut and her father. The latter ends up with Beaut having some success getting laboring men to "march" but to no clear end, certainly not the overthrow of capitalism.

Margaret is a "new woman," a beautiful and independent-minded Vassar graduate, but child of a pathetically weak and frustrated mother, Laura, and a domineering father. The father is a successful manufacturer. Like Margaret he is impressed with Beaut but knows that to keep his own control the young man may have to be destroyed. Ormsby would "crush the opposition," for "my kind of men always have to win" (309). The book ends with Ormsby saying to

Margaret, as part of his competition with Beaut for her loyalty, that women exist to create beauty, that's their role, and with neither of the Ormsbys really believing that for a minute. Margaret is very different from her mother, from Beaut's mother, from the pale woman with whom Beaut walks and talks in Coal Creek, and from Edith Carson. She either suggests a new kind of challenge for him, a true match at last, or a digression in the plot, since Anderson never goes on to resolve her role in the story.

Beaut cannot decide between Margaret and Edith, the frail and pale milliner defined by her genius for business and her frustrated yearning for love. Latching onto Beaut as the way out of a narrow, empty life, she pays for him to go to school, continues to serve him, then sees herself being displaced by the flashier and wealthier Margaret. Beaut, uncertain of his own motives, after her disappointment stops her from leaving town and in a bizarre scene—including Edith, Margaret, Beaut, and Ormsby—goes off with Edith. After that scene, however, Edith does not figure at all in the story.

Beaut meanwhile has started out as a shipping clerk in a warehouse, risen to foreman, quit, attended the University of Chicago, where he terrorized a professor whom he found all talk, no action and found fraternity boys beneath contempt, and finally studied for the law and been admitted to the bar. All this leads to one highly publicized murder trial in which Beaut, by means of an aggressive, ruthless defense, gets the innocent Andy Brown cleared of trumped-up charges. That is apparently his last court case, but it does connect Beaut with Margaret, who helps him win it, and it gives him the public profile he needs to begin to organize some men, to start his brigade of "marching" laborers.

Ever since Beaut wanted to organize the coal miners into an army, at least when not wanting to push them down a mine, his heroes have been Caesar, Alexander, Grant, and Sherman, that is, generals of armies. At moments, in Anderson's voice perhaps, he has compared his rage for order with the artist's passion for form. Men have been to him but counters in a game, things blown around in the world, with him the potential master-player. Alternatively he has been the drum-major of petty players in a marching band. All this may simply reflect Anderson's own feeling, as phrased in the novel, that "Something is wrong with modern American life" (100), that there is a "vacant, purposeless stare of modern life" (173). As bad as

Coal Creek is, Chicago in *Marching Men* is worse, "one vast gulf of disorder" (156), slovenly, squalid, full of men seeking fortunes with no sense of a dream or devotion, marked by soot, foul dust, and noisy streets. Beaut's landlady, who moved from Cairo with false hopes of the city as a place to realize dreams, represents to him "the miss-fire quality of much of American life" (77). For Beaut the opposing positive images are the cornfields, not only for their pastoral qualities so important to *Mid-American Chants* but also for the orderliness of ears in a row, and the Civil War, when men fought with purpose and discipline.

Beaut's obsession with marching platoons is only part of the story. Modern industrial capitalism, of course, has often depended in part on organizing persons as commodities in factories, on reducing them to functions. The labor movement, even as Anderson wrote, was—yes, through organizing them—helping workers gain more control over their own lives. Nowhere, however, does *Marching Men* suggest that the labor movement even exists. Nor does it imply that there are any particular goals that labor organized according to McGregor, and marching up and down the city, might achieve. "Brotherhood" is nonsense to Beaut, who anticipates that one day men will cease to be individuals. In fact, while Beaut articulates a disdain Anderson has for parts of modern American life, he also reflects Anderson's fear that America will breed Beaut McGregors—talented, charismatic, romantic, cruel—who will use their power to achieve frightening goals. More than once Beaut, for small cause, punches out people who irk him.

Just as Anderson can carry Sam McPherson through dissatisfaction with success and flight from responsibility, but does not conceptualize meaningful next stages in his life, so he can carry Beaut from rage for order and disdain for modern anomie to a kind of antiestablishment success, but he does not resolve either the political or the romantic lines of the story. Nor is it ever clear just what a more permanent relationship with Margaret or with Edith might mean, or what Beaut might do with his marching laborers, or where his anger will lead him or them or why. Because Anderson as writer is not a committed political activist, the frantic but unresolved nature of the book's ending is less a sign of political uncertainty than of the ambitiousness of his aspiration. As Mark Whalen's argument suggests, he was obsessed at this point, and during the ensuing war, with gender-based concerns about his ability to succeed as a writer, and Beaut's concerns with control are in line with Anderson's own passion.

"Mary Cochran"

Just as important to Anderson's literary growth as the two published early novels were two unpublished manuscripts, "Mary Cochran" and "Talbott Whittingham." He continued to rework both for some time, and did not give up on "Mary Cochran" until he cannibalized it for short stories in 1920 and 1921. "Mary Cochran," drafted in 1913, is the only one of Anderson's early extended manuscripts built around a female protagonist.[7] Like the others it is the story of an adolescent who strikes out for Chicago in search of a future. As a young woman, to be sure, Mary has few choices. She opts for secretarial work, although as the story progresses she has the spunk to secure a measure of control within her company. Mary's relationships with a series of men, however, become the primary theme, her career the secondary. She experiences frustration, desire, and loneliness, although the pattern in the series of relationships is not clear. As in the other novels individual episodes are striking even when a larger pattern is fuzzy.

Mary is the daughter of a New England physician and a Vaudeville singer who left her husband when Mary was an infant. She was "just not made" to be a village doctor's wife. Until the age of ten Mary lives with Cochran's cousin on an Ohio farm. After the doctor's death she moves to an Ohio college town until leaving for Chicago. When Mary finally does meet her mother, the latter has no interest in her and so Mary as a consequence loses one more romantic fantasy of her youth. When years later she returns to her New England village, she finds that a popular, slender girl who was tops in her high school class is now a fat slob, and that most of her classmates are unhappily married. Mary's epiphany is that girls and women are prepared for market like "little pigs" and trained to carry a sign, as it were, saying "See I am for sale." Mary realizes that she is actually glad to be single and uncaged. An alternative model is provided for her by Marion and Beatrice Wharton, tough-minded female owners of a printing company. By the end of Anderson's unfinished manuscript, Mary is a partner in Duke Yetter's company, has made improvements in it, and while married lives apart from her husband.

The man she marries, "Duke" Yetter, is one of several very different men who come into her life. In her youth she has a crush on Duke, known in her village as a rake, and she even writes him a love letter. She is devastated to overhear him boasting of the letter to his friends. On the rebound she falls for Carl Sorenson, a Swedish painter unhappily married to an academician. The relationship provides her first engagement with art, but Carl soon returns to his wife. In the Ohio college town Mary takes up with Emile Botts, a homely and awkward poet. Some of Anderson's most clumsy passages of prose occur when narrating and analyzing affairs between a man and a woman, and some of that prose is in "Mary Cochran." Emile writes poems that tell of his affection for Mary, who, incongruously, chases him through the woods feeling unworthy of such a majestic bard who has helped her see life in a new way. Then Emile becomes the aggressor, grabs her, and when she escapes sobs, "I shall always be unfit for the love of a woman" (49). Not surprisingly amid this pathos the manuscript breaks off to resume in Chicago with Mary now the chief secretary of Duke Yetter, tired, no longer either a virgin or a bold romantic but rather lonely, bored, and a willing partner in industry.

From this point on the two men in Mary's life are Duke Yetter and Sylvester Hunnicutt, although on the scene more briefly are also Lyof Sonareff, an unhappy Russian cobbler who desires Mary, and an unnamed Michigan salesman who has unrequited dreams about her. The primary counter to Yetter's strong male presence is Sylvester, a married man whose pipe-smoking wife, Gertrude, has been cheating him for years by doctoring the books on their Wisconsin poultry farm. The thematic tension in "Mary Cochran" to some extent from then on is based on Mary's alternating between Yetter and Sylvester, although at times she is on her own as in the return visit to New England.

Mary becomes the partner of Yetter, and also his wife, in the kind of two-residence marriage Anderson had with Tennessee Mitchell, and Sylvester writes a book on the "new woman." Apparently by this time Anderson realized that, while he had started to shift the theme to that of the "new woman," he had no idea what to do with Mary next and that Sylvester was at best a maudlin creation. He went no further. There are two other typescripts, with variations but no real advance in the story.

Sylvester, at the end an employee of Yetter, who also like Gertrude cheats him, is a dreamer with a gift for words, an honest man ("You are honest and yet you serve liars" [94], says Mary), and a storyteller, a kind of ironic persona for Anderson, one who seeks the rich smell of life and disdains middle-class values and beliefs. He not only makes the liberated argument that women are too often made to think of themselves merely as sex objects but also criticizes women for being too weak. He is also, however, the one who articulates the most sexist opinion of women's inferior passions and of their purely physical virtues, as against men's unification of social, scientific, and physical virtues. Sylvester fails in responding to Mary's passion, and finally, though she still "loves" him, she has no desire for sex with him. The climax of their relationship is a bizarre scene at the Wisconsin farm with Sylvester, Mary, Gertrude, and her frustrated foreman Doubtful Harcourt.

The abortive manuscript includes strong sections, some published as short stories such as "Unlighted Lamps." It is an attempt to adapt the paradigm of Anderson's other early novels to a woman's adventure. "Mary Cochran" also conveys Anderson's appreciation of the American girl's prescribed destiny as a commodity to be marketed. Satirically it pictures the "most popular" commodity in school as an unattractive adult years later. The manuscript suggests alternative roles and lifestyles for women through the picture of Marion and Beatrice as businesswomen in a two-woman partnership as an alternative to marriage, a partnership not necessarily sexual. Marriage, as is so often the case in Anderson's fiction, is not a happy state, but one might imagine a successful novella about Mary Cochran, a manuscript pruned of its excesses and developing further, with irony to be sure, her relationship with Duke Yetter into what Anderson might call a "successful" adjustment in the company. Mary would, in effect, albeit not acknowledged by Yetter, be the key to the success of the business.

"Talbott Whittingham"

Walter Rideout has been the most careful scholar of "Talbott Whittingham" and considers it the crucial manuscript in the author's growth toward *Winesburg*.[8] Written in 1914 and 1915, shortly before the earliest Winesburg tales, it has a significance hard to appreciate without wading through several hundred pages of manuscript material housed at the Newberry Library. Editing it will be a large task but one well worth doing even if not for print publication. One of the first challenges is to decide which "Talbott Whittingham" we are discussing. In addition to the story of Talbott the young painter from Bluefield, Ohio, who goes to New York for his career, there is a separate typescript of Talbott as a budding businessman and writer who grows up in the town of Mirage, Ohio, and moves to Chicago.

In the story of Talbott the artist only one part really focuses on his artistry, consisting mostly of a scene in a New York club with Talbott, Alexander Grayson, a wealthy steel magnate seeking to commission his own portrait, and a dealer named Bronson who has brought them together. That scene, however, intertwines with another, remembered from his youth, that has a significant impact on Talbott's art. In that episode Talbott, another youth, and two teenage girls go off to a secluded area on a "date" designed to lead to sex for both couples. The date for Talbott is Mazy Porters, daughter of a house painter, a girl who is a bit shy about going off to the barn with him. So they do not go, although in other scenes Talbott clearly is fascinated with young Mazy. Years later he paints a portrait of her, from memory and fancy, as a grand lady, "Lady Mazy of Kent," a gift for all women, the fantasy of a poor girl doing well. Juxtaposition of the Grayson scene and the Porters memory has a certain resonance, contrasting a sincere artistic impulse with painting for success and wealth, but also allowing Anderson to articulate his aesthetic of the significant impression and moment. As he recalls his last winsome view of Mazy, the moment that stood out in his mind when he painted her, he, or Anderson, reflects, "Life [is] full of such moments, when they are caught and held for a moment they become a part of life. What are you to do with them. If you are an artist you try to get the feel of them in your work."[9]

Anderson rewrote the Mazy Porters section many times, trying to get it right and apparently feeling it was crucial to his theme. In some drafts it is set in western New York State prior to Talbott's move to Ohio, but in most it is set in Bluefield, described as a small town in southeast Ohio. Sometimes Talbott is sixteen, sometimes fourteen. He is the son of a physician and lives with his widowed mother, although in another version the mother has died and he lives with his father, and in yet another the father is a judge. In several places Anderson notes that Talbott grew up in a "fashionable" part of town. In one version Talbott had a wife, Mary, who died in childbirth a year into the marriage. Other versions mention a late wife named Mildred or a wife named Sue Raymond, and a good bit of manuscript covers a marriage to Frances, mother of two children by Talbott.

What happens with the manuscript is what often happens to Anderson's novels in progress. Either because he has trouble taking his first story line further or because he has already planned a parallel narrative, he begins a second narrative. When he can connect the parts he has, for better or worse, a publishable text. In this case he never quite connects the strands. He does, however, experiment with narrative methods. In one long section, Anderson turns to an epistolary method with letters to "Ed," designated in different places as either Talbott's brother or a friend. Another whole section is full of Talbott's thoughts as a kind of interior monologue. At times there are developed scenes, at other times separate disconnected sentences. In one section, "Chapter Six," Anderson puts Talbott on a hill gaining a perspective on the land around and, metaphorically, on his past and his future.

In the pages with Talbott's thoughts is a good bit of narrative on Charlie Bristol, whose story actually takes up much of the overall manuscript. At one point Charlie tells Talbott his own story at length. There are hints of a homosexual relationship, but mostly through the gifts and hugs Charlie likes to give Talbott, as well as an early passage that asks, "Can a man love another man. It may be the only love that can exist." As Anderson develops the friendship, he has Talbott and Charlie attending college together, Dartmouth in fact, and a good bit of prose covers their college days. Talbott, in one version, was an excellent college athlete, particularly in baseball. The Chicago White Sox scouted him, and he dreamed of Grantland Rice and Ring Lardner writing about his heroics. The final parts of the manuscript are, in fact, about campus life, and at one point it is not clear whether Talbott is student or teacher.

The entire collection presents a fascinating case study of Anderson's methods, trying to find the right focus, the right techniques, to convey the experience of the protagonist with whom perhaps more than any other Anderson identified. He does seem to have settled at a certain point on the marriage with Frances and the two children being right for the story, although it is not clear why, and they do live in Cincinnati or on a farm near Cincinnati. When that strand cannot be developed further, however, Anderson narrates an affair Talbott had at twenty-three with an older woman named Kate. The affair covers several chapters but comes to an inconclusive finish in a country inn. All in all, however, the manuscripts reflect the neophyte novelist trying to connect art, sex, marriage, friendship, success, and a host of other concerns into a coherent text.

"Talbott Whittingham" is, as Rideout argues, probably the most important project in Anderson's early literary development. More profoundly than in *Windy McPherson's Son* and *Marching Men* he began to explore ways to craft experience and episode into coherent fiction, to use varied narrative techniques, to plumb character. He then apparently realized he had not and could not bring his project together. It was his attempt at a "Portrait of the Artist as a Young American," even though little of it is about art. The many lovers tried out for Talbott, from Mazy through hypothetical wives to Kate, suggest a strongly felt need to relate the theme of sexual or marital life to the theme of creative art, as either incompatible or not. The tie to Charlie Bristol suggests an alternative, but in every situation the communication and bond between humans is crucial for happiness even as such bonds can threaten the identity of the self and therefore the artist. Life and love are required for art, but threaten and are threatened by art, as money, or so that early Grayson scene implies, threatens art even as it is needed by the artist. One of Anderson's problems was his failure to bring coherence to the character of Charlie Bristol as either a foil or a satisfactory partner for Talbott. Anderson started Charlie's story in several ways but never seems to have clarified for himself what the nature of the character or his role in relation to Talbott should be.

Then there is the separate typescript of one Talbott Whittingham, the upstate New York boy sent at about twelve by his mother Mary Whittingham to live with friends in Mirage, Ohio, recalled nostalgically as a peaceful town with a stable that introduces Talbott to horses. He grows up there with Billy Bustard. The narrator is someone who has come to know Talbott but is not otherwise a character in the story. Talbott plays with a young girl, Janette Franks, who later gets pregnant and is forced against her wishes to marry the man who seduced her. Talbott's first sex, with a girl named Lillian Gale, is the subject of a chapter, and in another Kit Donohue, an Irish waitress, introduces the young man to smoke and drink.

At one point Talbott kills Billy's father, a paunchy bully who has been brutal to his son. Exonerated, Talbott takes off for Chicago, where he lives among artists, boxes with his friend Billows Turner (Talbott has earlier been described as an excellent athlete and ballplayer), and ends up as an advertising man. He also enjoys discussing Nietzsche and dreams of a "new army," in which the men are freed from inhibitions, fearless, and potential artists. By age twenty-nine he is also a writer. This typescript has more Chicago scenes, with a real feel of downtown streets and flats, than any of Anderson's other work. It comes to a curious end in a chapter that deals first with Talbott's relationship with one Adelaide Brown, a sophisticated but inhibited woman of thirty-two who likes artists, and then with one Lucile Bearing, a schoolteacher from Indiana, who takes her own life as Talbott watches. That moment, observing Lucile's ordeal and demise, seems, rather vaguely to be sure, to give Talbott a deeper sense of his artistic mission in life, as the portrait of Mazy in the other version more effectively suggests how an experience can be mediated into meaningful art. Or maybe it does not give him such a sense, for the typescript ends there. As Rideout says, however, the effort to tell the story of Talbott, which must have taken an enormous amount of Anderson's time in 1914 and 1915, was very important to developing the strengths of *Winesburg, Ohio*. The emphasis on capturing the moment or impression, the attempt to reveal, impressionistically, the buried life, considering the significance of point of view, the relationship between an action and the observer's, or the artist's, perspective on it and how it is turned into art—in these areas and others Anderson grew as a result of his work on "Talbott Whittingham."

MID-AMERICAN CHANTS AND *A NEW TESTAMENT*

In 1918, following Anderson's novels and shortly before *Winesburg, Ohio* appeared in bookstores but while some of its tales were being published, John Lane Company brought out *Mid-American Chants*, an eighty-two-page collection of verse. Nine years later Anderson published his only other book of poetry, *A New Testament*. Anderson is not a significant figure in the history of American poetry. One might compare Faulkner, whose two collections of verse get lost in any discussion of his career. There is, nonetheless, more poetic sensibility and craft in *The Marble Faun* and *A Green Bough* than in Anderson's poetry, albeit a rather pale, decadent sensibility, and Faulkner before shifting to fiction had started out thinking of poetry as his chosen genre. Anderson, like other writers, may have considered poetry the first among arts, but he never seems to have had a phase during which he thought of himself as primarily a poet.

Mid-American Chants, however, does reflect Anderson's romantic belief in the role of a peculiarly American poet-writer-artist, his belief that the story of America and particularly of the Midwest, must be sung, even if not by him. Like Carl Sandburg, Anderson imitates and echoes Walt Whitman as his bardic hero, but he also apologizes for his region of the country. The Midwest is still too immersed in the practical affairs of economic development to have a great poetry, an argument heard a century before about the United States itself. The singer needs "something that is very old" in his culture to develop a mature voice, "memory haunted places" not found in midwestern "towns and fields," full of "steaming coal heaps," the "grinding roar of machines," and "the terrible engine—industrialism" (7–8).[10] One might be hearing Henry James explaining why literature in the United States is not yet a rich literature. Anderson seeks tolerance for "this book of chants" as he tries "to express the hunger within." Perhaps "they may find an answering and clearer call in the hearts of other Mid-Americans." All his life he remained self-consciously the son of "Mid-America," a very different place from the East.

Anderson frequently uses free-verse lines in *Mid-American Chants*, whereas the "poems" in *A New Testament* are largely prose paragraphs. In both books a shifting kaleidoscopic "I" speaks, in the earlier collection imitating the voice in Whitman's "Song of Myself," in the later volume less anchored to any particular self or significance. Most of the motifs in *Mid-American Chants* appear in its opening piece, "The Cornfields," a set of eight prose paragraphs. Cornfields and corn are dominant images throughout the book, suggesting the Midwest and its fertile fields, but also drawing on older traditions of sexuality and fertility and usually representing the positive alternative to images of war, death, and industrialism. The poem, although in prose paragraphs, reads as a chant and might as easily be in lines. The rhythms, lacking variety, may have more in common with rap music than with folk songs.

"The Cornfields" opens, "I am pregnant with song." The "I," spirit of midwestern life, will, because people are "bound with chains" and have forgotten the fields and corn and "west winds," "renew in my people the worship of gods" (11). The god or gods, it seems, the "sacred vessel" as well, will emerge from the cornfields. The second poem is called "Chicago," but it is neither like Sandburg's "hog butcher of the world" with a crude and coarse magnetism nor like Whitman's "Keep your splendid silent sun" praising the city equally with the country. Rather it is "old and palsied," "dying," yet ironically "at the beginning of my life" and too young to sing and know the words (13). "Chicago" is then followed by "Song of Industrial America," an America broken not celebrated, "ugly and brutal" not something positive. Unlike Whitman, Anderson cannot sing the praises of his urban world, and in a letter to Babs Finley in October 1917 he explicitly contrasts midwestern cornfields with "ugly" city streets.[11] The poem "Manhattan" ennobles not the city but the western cornfields. In another poem the speaker says, "Let the factories close and the voices die./Let me sing now" (35). And he will sing of corn and the "throne of gods."

There are forty-nine poems, some very short, but again and again they describe cornfields, at times presented with both sexual and religious significance. They often mention Chicago, negatively but not without implying some hope for a better future for American cities, one not defined by dehumanizing factories and deracinated lives. Toward the end there are references to the Great War just ended. In just about all cases the "I" is the chanter, the singer still seeking his voice and song, still trying to bring some mysterious value associated with the cornfields to the modern urban world of industrial America. There is some of Sandburg here but also some of Vachel Lindsay and even of the more pensive melancholy of Edgar Lee Masters. Underneath it all is a pastoral vision but one whose long-term implications the writer has not fully considered.

A New Testament, published in 1927 by Liveright, is, as the title implies, an attempt to present a different kind of scripture, one whose religious references are limited. Most of the book consists of individual sketches and portraits a bit like those found in *Winesburg, Ohio—*

"The Man with the Trumpet," "A Young Man," "A Dreamer," "The Dumb Man," "A Thinker," and so forth. Usually the "I" is the self being portrayed. "The Story Teller" is reprinted from *The Triumph of the Egg* (1921), but reflects the overall pathos and melancholy of the book, since the narrator is a helpless man" watching "tales" that are "people who sit on the doorstep of the house of my mind," often "dying of cold and hunger."[12] The poems were written over several years, stretching back to the time of *Mid-American Chants,* and do not specifically reflect Anderson's mind in 1926 and 1927. They do reflect his interest in "the Negro" from the earlier 1920s, in poets and artists, in vagrants and dreamers, in old men and young men, in the West. They do not have the consistent theme of *Mid-American Chants* but rather a consistent melancholy tone, almost as if George Willard were editing the sketches years after leaving Winesburg and after learning that life beyond the village also has a sadness that resonates beyond the hopes spurring young people off to cities, ambition, and careers.

3

Literary Success

THE TURN IN ANDERSON'S CAREER WAS HIS REALIZATION THAT HE
had a genius for the short prose form, in particular the impressionistic sketch and the tale rather than the traditional "short story." He
continued to write novels, but his best writing was always in tales,
sketches, essays, or discrete parts of autobiographical books. The
book for which he has been most admired, *Winesburg, Ohio*, succeeds
because of individual pieces and their cumulative impact but also because while it was a very personal book for Anderson he found a
technique that gave him artistic control over the personal themes.

The genesis of the tales in *Winesburg*—beginning with "The Book
of the Grotesque," "Hands," "Queer," and "Paper Pills" in late 1915
and early 1916—is best told in Ray Lewis White's comprehensive introduction to his scholarly edition of the book.[1] White incorporates
Anderson's own later recollections of its genesis, what we can infer
from manuscripts and correspondence, the role played by such early
prose pieces as "The New Note" and "Sister" and "The Story Writers"
in shaping his thoughts about art, and the influence of Anderson's
Chicago friends and environment on the development of his craft.[2]
White also clarifies the evolution of the order of the stories: the first
five were pretty well set in place from the start of Anderson's ar-
rangement of the book, but others were shuffled, and the foreword,
with its new name, was put in place later. One crucial development,
of course, was, John Lane Company having cut its ties to the author,
making a connection with Ben Huebsch, who became the publisher
for Anderson's next six books.[3]

The twenty-two pieces in *Winesburg* have been organized by critics into diverse patterns. "The Book of the Grotesque" is like an overture expressing themes to be developed later, although the opening story, "Hands," also functions well as an overture. The final narrative, George Willard's departure by train, seems to complete a theme in the text, George's maturation, although there is critical debate over how much George has changed. Many tales cover problems of communication, lonely persons, repressions, obsessions, fantasies, or people who are designated as "different" or weird in some way. Most focus on a single individual, although his or her problem may only be clarified through a relationship or interaction with George or someone else. What structure there is to the book grows out of cumulative effects, repeated motifs, and a consistent tone rather than a line of development in character or plot. The method of the book, in fact, is similar to that "mythopoeic" method that Benjamin Spencer years ago traced as a key to appreciating Anderson—a probing for the essence of things, as well as a concern with the intuitive, the mystic, the archetypal, and forces beyond the phenomenal.[4]

David Anderson has shown over and over that *Winesburg* is not a cardinal text in the revolt against the village or small town often seen as a common pattern in early twentieth-century American literature.[5] The book is bleak and is set in a village, pathetic bleak rather than tragic or violent bleak, but the narrowness of the characters' lives is not a peculiar consequence of village life. In Anderson's early novels small-town settings are portrayed negatively, but the cities to which characters move are no better. Clarence Lindsay argues that Anderson's strength, in fact, derives in part from his commitment to "staying home" in the Midwest small town, that both his formal innovations and his peculiar genius and insight are tied to his dedication to exploring small-town experiences. The writer himself, in fact, once said, "I belong in little towns."[6] As Anderson continued, moreover, mechanization and standardization became the villain, and cities showed up as more stultifying than villages. It is also likely that Anderson developed some of his material for *Winesburg* from people he met and situations he witnessed in Chicago as well as from experiences in Clyde or other Ohio villages. The book, nonetheless, is set in a village or small town, and readers can only form a depressing conception of life in that town from the information provided. At the same time they cannot really infer a positive alternative, in the

city or elsewhere, from anything in the text, and in at least one letter
from the period Anderson described Chicago as a "horrible" place,
a city of "the dead."[7]

George Willard is the closest thing in *Winesburg, Ohio* to a lead
character, hardly a protagonist, rather a listener or foil for someone
else except in the episodes of sexual activity or courtship with Louise
Trunion or Belle Carpenter or Helen White and in "Departure." Anderson therefore can finesse the difficulty he faced in his early novels, and indeed in later ones as well, of trying to develop a main
character conceptually, beyond superficial traits, and through life
changes. George can have vague dreams, physical urges, and an
openness that encourages others to talk to him; but George is not a
complex character. As a central device for this fictional text, however, he is a brilliant strategy.

"The Book of the Grotesque," the earliest of the pieces to be written but not originally designed to open the book, suggests that
Winesburg, Ohio will consist of a gallery of grotesque forms, persons
warped in one way or another. In one sense this is true. At least fourteen characters are repressed or warped or unusually odd due in
some way to their earlier experiences. "The Book of the Grotesque,"
as written by the old man, however, describes the "grotesque" as
what happens when a person allows a single truth of the many inter-
woven truths in the world to dominate him, to obsess him. Only the
story "Godliness" deals strictly with that kind of distortion. The
other theme of "The Book of the Grotesque," the writer-carpenter
as craftsman, pregnant with the procession of figures (grotesques)
who can be amusing and even beautiful, does anticipate what follows—the rich suggestiveness of a sequence of characters whose
often pathetic lives can still be formed into an amusing, meaningful
beauty.

It is Wing Biddlebaum, né Adolph Myers of Pennsylvania, whose
story, "Hands," best prefaces what is to follow. In Winesburg he is little known and generally ignored. In his hometown he was an inspired, dedicated schoolteacher, encouraging students to be ambitious, to fulfill their boyhood dreams. Too free with his hands in
touching the children he inspired, he became victim first of a half-
wit's accusations, then of other lads echoing the dubious charges in
a scenario that alludes to the Salem witch trials. When beaten by a
townsman and threatened with lynching, Myers fled to Ohio and be-

came Biddlebaum, never to teach again. What may surprise one upon rereading is the reminder that he was but twenty when driven out of town and, indeed, is only forty now when he is nonetheless described as a fat little *old* man, a frightened outsider who still talks best with his hands until in horror he pushes them back into his pockets. Only George, about the same age Wing was during his crisis, reaches out to this picture of loneliness who at table may remind one of a priest at his rosary.

Isolation and loneliness recur in *Winesburg*. Sexual motifs, as either a critique of American sexual obsessions or an exploration of marital problems, also recur in stories of Mother, Dr. Reefy, Joe Welling, Alice Hindman, Wash Williams, Curtis Hartman, Kate Swift, Enoch Robinson, and Ray Pearson. The difficulty of following one's dream is also a recurrent theme. Wing Biddlebaum, that is, anticipates much of what follows, and the continuing resonance of "Hands" lies as much in its importance to the whole of *Winesburg* as in its strength as a tale.

Dr. Reefy is also an "old man," but since he was forty-five when marrying the pregnant young victim of a village seducer he is at least close to sixty now. In "Paper Pills" Reefy communicates less well through speech than with his hands, marked by knuckles the size of walnuts, and with little scraps of paper on which he writes messages, messages never revealed in the story. As grotesque as Wing, Reefy once read these messages to his wife but now merely scrunches them into round balls. Whether they are the wisdoms of fortune cookies, tired clichés, or "little pyramids of truth" (14) one never knows. More central to the story is that Reefy, although he has a friend, John Spaniard, never again really reached out to a person as he once had to the young woman. Never again that is until Elizabeth Willard visits him prior to her death.

Elizabeth is a scarred person, old at forty-one and ill. Unlike Reefy's youth, Elizabeth's is told. She was always the outsider, a bit "star-struck," living without family love in the hotel and asserting her identity by donning men's clothes and by a flaunted looseness with traveling salesmen. Trapped in an unhappy marriage in the shabby hotel, she devotes herself to her promising son, George, prays for his happiness, that he be neither "drab" nor overly "smart," and despises her handsome, selfish husband, Tom, who, also out of touch, dreams of one day being governor of Ohio.

At the end of the book, in a tale set earlier than "Paper Pills," Anderson brings these two lonely people together, but allows them no fulfillment. They talk, of life and love, of the blind seeking so common to people, and they kiss but then part. Elizabeth dies, known to most as a hysterical old woman, but the location of her eight-hundred-dollar savings, behind the bedroom wall, is never known by anyone else. The pathos of her early death is intensified by the conflicted response of son George, our "hero" and her idol, a response consisting of guilt, relief, and—as a defense mechanism—even annoyance that the death will keep him from having a date with Helen White.

The opening tales establish atmosphere, themes, style, and motifs that help bring the parts of the book together. Most of the tales, except for "Godliness" and "Tandy" and a few about George himself, follow similar patterns and cumulatively develop a gallery of odd and lonely villagers as provocative as those in Edwin Arlington Robinson's Tilbury and more poignant than those in Edgar Lee Masters's Spoon River. Some, such as Alice Hindman, Tom Foster, Curtis Hartman, and Kate Swift are passive and repressed. Others, such as Wash Williams, Joe Welling, Seth Richmond, Enoch Robinson, and Elmer Cowley, take more aggressive action even though isolated and pathetic figures, losers in the eyes of their fellow townspeople.

A word first about "Godliness," the sixth tale and really a four-chapter novella. To Marc Conner "Godliness" is a "vivid representation" of the central struggle in the book, the son's working through of a complex relationship with the father. Not disconnected from the structure of Winesburg as many argue, it "forms the defining pattern of the entire collection" and was crucial to Anderson's resolution, from vicarious patricide to vicarious reconciliation we might say, of his own perspective on Irwin Anderson.[8] In the story Jesse Bentley, the only Civil War survivor of five brothers, is called home from a Presbyterian seminary to run the family farm. His own wife dies soon, of hard work, leaving him with one child, Louise. Warped by her upbringing and neurotic, the pathetic Louise marries a man named John Hardy and bears one child, David. Jesse is a religious fanatic, but perhaps more driven by lust to own all the nearby land and establish like Abraham a patriarchal line than by a mission to convert anyone to Christ. The narrator rather tongue-in-cheek contrasts his own secular-materialist worldview with Jesse's evangelical worldview and belief that God will give him a sign that his wealth is holy. The story's two pivotal episodes are Jesse's mad plea for a sign from God, a plea that frightens young David, and Jesse's attempt to sacrifice either a lamb or David in the forest, a terrifying scene that drives David at fifteen forever away from Winesburg. Conflating the Isaac and Goliath stories, David flees the patriarch after first hitting him in the head with a stone from his slingshot, whether fatally or not is never revealed.

Like none of the other tales in the book, "Godliness" nonetheless epitomizes the old carpenter's motif, captures the warped quality of Winesburg experience, anticipates George's flight not from fanaticism but depressing sterility, vividly develops the father-son conflict (even if through a grandfather) so well outlined by Marc Conner as a central concern of the book, and repeats the theme of human failure at communication. Almost all the other stories are of townspeople like Dr. Reefy and Dr. Percival, the exceptions being those that deal with George's groping for sexual maturity and "Tandy," a curio about a little girl who represents the promise of youth to be special, to be a real self, to be different.

Dr. Percival, ironically "the philosopher," is a fat, black-toothed, unclean, odd cigar-smoker, son of an insane father, a raconteur who enjoys telling his tales to George, a doctor with few patients, and overall an unpleasant person. Having spent his youth as a pious Christian and good son while his brother was an ungrateful drunkard, Percival now, the drunken brother having been killed by a train, has become a somewhat paranoid misanthrope filling George with contempt for human beings. If Percival is not crazy, there is at least no love, no shared relationship, in his life. The misanthropy has no clear cause, his brother's death perhaps signifying the wages of sin, and it is strangely accompanied by a message that "everyone in the world is Christ and they are all crucified" (35), a philosophy suggesting a cynicism in the face of the universality of death and a self-pity that the common human fate is undeserved, perhaps even that the creator-father of such a world must have been as insane as his own father. When Percival refuses to treat a girl run over by a buggy and, unknown to him, actually dead, he fears a lynch mob, a mob that might bring about his own destiny to be crucified.

The reader never learns more about Percival's fate, nor is it perhaps important to know more. In fact only rarely does Anderson provide any sense of the long-term fate of his characters or a broader sense of the town from which these grotesques are estranged. Wing was beaten up in Pennsylvania not Ohio. Rather we see them in their isolation or in rare relationships, and while their stories are integrally tied to the village setting their problems in some ways are as true of city life as village life.

The women in Winesburg, at least the older women, not Helen or Belle, are all marked by sexual motifs—Elizabeth's looseness as a teenager, Alice's one-time affair with a man who leaves her and never returns, Kate's suggestively mysterious past. Alice Hindman is so foolishly steadfast in expecting her lover's return and then so resigned to her situation that she can never develop a meaningful life for herself. She joins the church at twenty-five, runs out naked one night in the rain, but cannot even bring herself to accept the affection of bumbling but kind Will Hurley, the drug clerk with a fancy for her. Her one-time lover is not really portrayed as a villain in this tale, nor justified, for it is not his tale. Alice is just a stunted creature, too fragile to get over the sadness.

Kate Swift is a stronger woman, one defined by her beautiful features and figure but pockmarked complexion, by impulsive passions and a character at once stern and forbidding, then happy and talkative, then affectionate to George, whom she allows briefly to caress her. Having been to New York and Europe and having adopted the habit of smoking, although not in public, she is more sophisticated than others in Winesburg. Lying in bed she attracts through her window the gaze of Rev. Curtis Hartman, a forty-year-old frustrated in his marriage to a stout, nervous, passionless woman. Ironically, as the reticent Presbyterian preacher is lusting after "another woman" ("I shall give myself over to sin" [131], he says), that woman, Kate, is praying by her bed. In another of Anderson's strange conclusions, Hartman then claims to George that he has "found the light" (133). At the end of "The Teacher," he comes upon Kate and George as they part, and one rather hopes that a pending conversation between Kate and Hartman does not lead anywhere. Although none of the characters in *Winesburg* is complex in the way the term describes richly developed characters in novels, Kate suggests a more diverse set of associations and evokes a more diverse set of responses than most other characters in the book. Chris Browning considers her the author's "portrait of his ideal woman," but Belinda Bruner is closer to the mark in describing Kate as one of George's most effective teachers, in effect "a martyr to the cause of unrequited teaching."[9] While Bruner understates the irony in Hartman's lust for Kate, which she calls "a holy vision leading him out of spiritual despair," she well conveys the conflicted feelings within both Kate and George that in effect utilize the erotic as positive "pedagogical force," one that has a deeper impact than do the lessons of George's first "teacher" in the book, Wing Biddlebaum.

Meanwhile Anderson develops a gallery of curious male villagers. Joe Welling, a Standard Oil agent described as "A Man of Ideas," is also a "little volcano" (81) bursting into excited talk when a topic stimulates him. His bizarre trait saves his skin when his beloved's male family members, who today would be described as "bad dudes all," come to assault Joe and are stunned into a retreat by his wild yammering over a "new vegetable kingdom" (89). Another grotesque, Wash Williams, a huge, ugly, and filthy telegraph operator, once had a tall blonde wife in Dayton. She took lovers. He sent her packing. Then when her mother, to reconcile them, pushed the wife into the living room naked, Wash in a rage hit her with a chair and fled. Since Wash lives at Willard's Hotel, he seems meant to be a representative resident of that narrow world where Elizabeth and George have both grown up. Anderson, as he so often does, marks his warped characters with grotesque features, in Wash's case a bloated face, thin neck, feeble legs, and dirtiness. Wash's misogyny, the rage that all women are "foul," is not Anderson's but the author, rarely writing of happy affairs or marriages, does frequently portray lovers as betrayed by unfaithful spouses and wooers.

Seth Richmond, "The Thinker," like George has a crush on Helen White, and indeed is even conned into playing John Alden to his Myles Standish, but remains a self-pitying outsider, smart enough, he feels, to know that George is "a fool" but unable to gain the respect of anyone but his own mother, his father having died in a street fight with a Toledo newsman. Also smitten by Helen White is Tom Foster, a gentle quiet loafer who turns to drink, silently harboring his hopeless love. Alcohol and the occasional prostitute are all he has left. From story to story, character to character, the connections between the erotic and the artistic, between sexual and communicative frustration, between agency and identity freed from, albeit as Conner suggests reconciled with, the father—these connections develop as leitmotifs that give *Winesburg, Ohio* its great resonance as a fictional symphony of small-town American life.[10]

In the same town is Enoch Robinson, who fled a wife and children in Brooklyn and has landed in Winesburg lonely and unfulfilled. He is an awkward and lame boy-man who once had artistic skills but never any real understanding of self or world. Just as pathetic is Elmer Cowley, "Queer," son of a merchant. Like Enoch, Elmer sees George as an insider belonging, unlike himself, in the town. He remains not only a newcomer but also condemned to be without friends. Desiring to be like others and self-conscious over being seen as queer, he can communicate only with Monk, a half-wit farm worker. Elmer cannot even talk with George but, as he gets ready to flee town by train, he suddenly starts hitting George over and over, cries out, "I guess I showed him I aint so queer" (178), and then leaves, not, however, without first returning twenty dollars he had stolen from his father's store.

These are the kinds of characters who people George's village. Some interact with George, a few with real communication. George himself really is more mature by the time of the penultimate tale, "Sophistication," when he and Helen do communicate effectively. He feels "they had for a moment taken hold of the thing that makes the mature life of men and women in the modern world possible" (218). They have come to grips with the realization that there is no ultimate meaning to life, but they also appreciate the joy of vitality itself and learn, as the once arch-romantic Emerson did, that "in popular experience, everything good is on the highway" not at the end of the rainbow or in a transparent eyeball.[11] Like the county fair with which "Sophistication" begins, it is a time of both ambition and regret, ghosts and voices of the past, grace and beauty and promise of a future. Although *Winesburg* has not narrated George's growth and maturity, this tale, placed after Mother's death and before George's departure, suggests that he has matured and is ready for a future, a future about which we are not to be told but a future that implicitly might benefit from all that the young man has learned from interactions with the people of his hometown. Perhaps, as Conner suggests, he goes forth to tell the stories of his hometown grotesques, for at times it does seem that they are hoping he can, much as Quentin Compson in Faulkner's *Absalom, Absalom!* at least for a while believes that Rosa Millard wants him to go forth to tell her story to a wider audience.

Winesburg, Ohio remains the most optimistic book-length fiction of Anderson's about its main character, even if it remains depressing about the world of the book itself. It was also a rare successful attempt to craft a book-length fiction that does not peter out into a vague or silly or unconvincing final section. It succeeds because Anderson exploited his strengths in the short impressionistic sketch, because he wrote out of deep personal concerns about family and identity and career, and because he combined these strengths and this probing with an effective orchestration of motifs and repeated patterns and moods that results in a more resonant and suggestive overall tapestry than he ever achieved again. Also central to the book's success was the discovery of a main character, George, who did not have to be the traditional protagonist of a novel but could be a mirror and sounding board for a gallery of village figures making up that tapestry and could also grow from that experience and go forth at the end, perhaps still young and naïve but well prepared for new adult adventures. Although, as Marcia Jacobson effectively argues, the ending does not clearly show George as a mature adult, but still as an adolescent with an undefined future, it does imply the possibility of a bright future without the baggage other Anderson characters carry at the end of their stories.[12]

POOR WHITE

Unlike Anderson's post-*Winesburg* novels, his early novels and manuscripts focus on a young person's quest to confront his or her world and make something of him- or herself. They are designed as growing-up narratives. The novels of the 1920s are tales of middle-aged crises, and the final novel is quite different in form from all the earlier ones. *Poor White* is a product of a transitional phase in Anderson's career, when he has concluded *Winesburg*, is writing some of his best stories, and is soon to be rated as one of the best writers in America. Some scholars call it his best novel. It is his only novel to focus on a larger community rather than a single character or two characters. Hugh McVey, to be sure, is another in Anderson's line of young-man protagonists, but Anderson gradually shifts his focus from Hugh to changes taking place in the town of Bidwell.

Poor White is set in a clearly historical past, the last two decades of the nineteenth century. Much American fiction published around

1920—for example, Edith Wharton's *The Age of Innocence*, Sinclair Lewis's *Main Street*, Willa Cather's *My Antonia*—was concerned with social change, often nostalgically, from the perspective of the present. Anderson sets his progressive town of Bidwell three decades earlier, when he himself was maturing, but is also concerned about the changes in American life at the time he is writing. He is distressed by the loss of a sense of craftsmanship in manufacturing, by the misperceptions surrounding genius and success, by the disruption of gender relationships, and by the seeming crassness of the new economy.

Until Hugh McVey arrives in Bidwell, *Poor White* is designed much as Anderson's earlier novels had been. A young man becomes impatient with his life in a village, strikes out on the open road passing through several states, and lands in a larger town where he achieves some success. Like Coal Creek, Mudcat Landing is a miserable place to be born, a hole of a town whose nearby land is arid and worthless, a town full of exhausted, no-account, gaunt men and merchants who cannot even pay for their goods. There is nostalgia in Anderson's fiction but never for the places where his characters actually grow up.

Hugh McVey is Anderson's rewriting of another Missouri idler, Huckleberry Finn, although with just enough vague ambition to suggest Tom Sawyer as well. The allusions are several. At fourteen Hugh is tall, uneducated, lazy, and unmannered, and he has a dreamy outlook on life. He most enjoys the indolence that prevails at his father's fishing shack but hates his slothful, greasy father. Father is the town drunkard, a widower, seen by most as a bum on the streets, a onetime tanner who now occasionally sweeps saloons or cleans cisterns. Hugh has his own Widow Douglas/Miss Watson, a frugal New Englander named Sarah Shepard who moved west in 1866, educates Hugh, and encourages him to be energetic and ambitious. She hopes he will be better than "poor white trash" (14), thus the book's title.[13]

When Sarah and her husband, after five years, do leave Hugh's village, Hugh is torn between a native indolence and that vague ambition stirring in him, as Anderson seems to define it between his shiftless southern hill heritage and the spirit of Sarah's Yankee teachings. When at twenty he leaves his position as stationmaster in Mudcat Landing, unlike Huck he does not light out for the territory or, following Horace Greeley's advice, go west to success, but rather, like

Willa Cather's Jim Burden, he heads east, to the land of dreams for a new generation.

The rest of Book One covers Hugh's travels through Iowa, Illinois, Indiana, and Ohio. The river, particularly at night, as it does for Huck Finn, provides Hugh with a vehicle for dreaming, for separating himself from the world of men even while feeling part of something bigger. Two hours in Chicago convey the message that cities, where people are like insects, machines rule, and a newcomer gets lost in the whirling, churning mass of humanity, provide no answer for Hugh or for Anderson. The towns through which he wanders, moreover, seem all alike. This tall ungainly youth feels "queer" as he overhears conversations about America's potential, the ideas of Thomas Paine and Edward Bellamy, and books he has not read.

When Hugh arrives in Bidwell the novel changes directions and Hugh's role in it also changes. His character has been protean enough to allow for some reshaping of his role, and, in effect, now he becomes the odd, separated, dreamy telegraph operator and crazy inventor. More importantly he also becomes the object of the town's mythmaking as a brilliant genius, even, so some believe, a superman-captain-of-industry in the making. Hugh therefore functions as a device for Anderson to satirize not only the gullibility of people who create false heroes but also the distortions found in his own earlier profession of public relations. Hugh is an active character only in relation to his curious inventions and his even more curious courtship of and marriage to Clara Butterworth, though even there his role is more passive than active.

Otherwise Hugh as a developing character is of less interest to Anderson and the reader. After his books' opening parts, the same thing happens to Anderson's other early protagonists—Sam McPherson after his business success, Beaut McGregor except for the bizarre quality of his extreme behavior, surely Mary Cochran and Talbott Whittingham, when Anderson ran out of ideas for them. Anderson was at his best with impressionistic insights into character, not development of full portraits. He effectively uses George Willard as a kind of *ficelle* in *Winesburg, Ohio,* and at the end of his career he achieves a certain success in *Kit Brandon* by focusing on the way she is seen and interpreted by an older male narrator rather than by developing her character directly. *Poor White* is actually a better book because Anderson does change his focus at the start of Book Two.

Bidwell becomes the landscape for depicting what Anderson sees as a significant change in American society. Unlike Winesburg it is a prosperous place in a river valley, with good soil, the railroad, crowds milling in town on clear evenings, happy couples, and a sense of impending change, of waiting, of seeking, of talking about new times, of getting on in the world. The cast of characters is broad. Peter White, the tailor, is a wife-beater, yet women in town sympathize with him. Alice Mulberry, the "half-wit," is also a whittler. Jane Orange, a rich but stingy widow, is caught stealing eggs. Judge Horace Hanby, formerly a governor in the South, is a scoundrel who predicts coming class warfare. Joseph Wainsworth is a harness maker and dedicated craftsman. Tension between Joseph and his boorish and less conscientious assistant, Jim Gibson, becomes thematically significant. There are also Ed Hall, the carpenter, and Ezra French, the cabbage farmer, and others.

In some ways *Poor White* is a counterargument to *Winesburg, Ohio*, composed as Anderson's personal reaction to his own portrayal of a small Ohio town as boring, repressive, and stagnant. Bidwell at the same general historic time is bustling, changing, full of opportunity, and anticipating new forces at work in the United States. Not only can people talk about personal matters to one another, they communicate a lot. Anderson may be as skeptical about the ultimate drift of the town as he was about Winesburg, but Bidwell has vitality and a sense of a new force "replacing individualism," he adds with irony. In the New Age, probably an age without poetry as *Mid-American Chants* also implied, merchants and industrialists and capitalist princes are glorified, and the new forces promise to seal people together in a new order. For Anderson, the romantic individualist, the two greatest enemies to the individual are the modern drive to be part of something bigger—whether a populist fascism as represented by Beaut McGregor's drives or an industrialized consumerism run by Morgan, Frick, Carnegie, Vanderbilt, and their ilk—and the inability of the isolated, lonely individuals, those of a Winesburg, to communicate, to reach beyond themselves, and to grow.

In the nervous world of Bidwell, Hugh McVey is a timid, queer, lonely, dreamy telegraph operator who nonetheless is, ironically, perceived by townsmen as a symbol of the New Age. His fantasies and frustrations, to be sure, are what lead him to a series of inventions that reinforce his iconic role—a machine to plant cabbages, a coal-car unloader, a corn-cutter. To a great extent, however, once Hugh is mystified as a genius Anderson pays little attention to him as a character. He redirects the book toward Steve Hunter, Clara and Tom Butterworth, and townspeople like Joe Wainsworth. Hugh when seen generally acts strangely, waving his arms in a cabbage field or hugging his machine. It is Steve who drives the action in the story of Bidwell's industrial adventure, who aspires to leadership in a new movement, who worships captains of industry as supermen. It is also Steve who mystifies Hugh as a genius and sees Hugh as the key to his own future as "the one great man of the community" (113). Like other Americans of his generation, remarks the old advertising man Anderson, Steve does not know that reputations are made like an automobile, that to some extent "great men" are mere illusions "sprung out of a national hunger for greatness," that politicians, bankers, and railroad men "employ men to glorify" them (95–97). Neither Steve nor Hugh is employing a public relations agent, but to Anderson the public image of anyone involved in the New Age is probably a far cry from reality.

Steve is a crude entrepreneur, who begins to think of other people as puppets, a shrewd small-town survivor but hardly an "embryo industrial magnate" like his heroes (112). When the cabbage planter turns out to be a failure, Steve lies effectively enough to keep the worst news from shareholders while he and Hugh are making a profit on the coal-car unloader. As important as Steve's relationship to Hugh, however, is the tension between Steve and Tom Butterworth, the "old" power in Bidwell. Butterworth's wealth and power were tied to his land holdings, although now he is more businessman than farmer. The actual extent of Tom's influence in the age of fluid capital remains vague, and very soon the book's focus shifts to tensions between Tom and his daughter Clara, one of Anderson's attempts at the "New Woman." So while it is clear that Tom is a boastful big shot, growing fat in middle age and losing the lean hardness that made him a success, he is otherwise presented simply as what Steve is replacing as the mover and shaker in Bidwell.

Much of the second half of the novel focuses on Clara. Anderson develops Clara's story in parallel with Hugh's, a woman and a man groping for identity in a changing world. The pattern also suggests a recurring concern of Anderson with the relationship between gender relations and male success. Sam McPherson achieves success in business, but once he marries the boss's daughter his drives and hers become incompatible; as a consequence, it would seem, both Sam and the author lose direction. Beaut McGregor is more frightening but seems headed in some direction until Margaret Ormsby takes over the book, or one might say until Beaut's uncertainty between staying loyal to Edith Carson or tying himself to Margaret becomes Anderson's focus. The novel then fizzles out. In both cases, Sue and Margaret, the woman involved is a "New Woman." Much of Anderson's fiction remains deeply conflicted on gender issues. He had found unfulfilling a traditional marriage with children and a regular job, and then he stumbled through two shorter marriages with different kinds of "New Women." He tried to take seriously the issues faced by women of his day, and if he never really developed a convincingly complex female portrayal, well, he never really developed a convincingly complex male character either.[14]

Although Anderson may have had trouble resolving story lines that included a male-female relationship and the separate portrayal of the female character's story, there is an increasing sensitivity in his characterizations of Sue, Margaret, Mary Cochran, and then Clara. Clara is the fullest character of all, and as Hugh has been set aside during the middle of the novel, her story takes over. Only later does Anderson bring Hugh back as an unlikely husband for the strong, tall, attractive Clara. She hates her domineering father, more than she hated young John May, who tried to ravish her. Tom has never been sensitive to his motherless daughter's needs, and he violates "something very precious in her nature" (156). Jim Priest, the old hand on the farm, is in her eyes a substitute father in this gross, ugly world of vulgar men and animals, and responds to her need for understanding and friendship. She even has fantasies of Jim as a young lover (147).

Clara goes off to college at Ohio State, and while the McVey-Hunter saga continues in Bidwell, the book focuses on her in Columbus. There is no mention of anything she studies in class or any career toward which she aspires. Ohio State simply sets her apart from the Bidwell story. The only goal she can imagine is getting married: "what else can a woman do?" (190). In Columbus, however, she feels, as Mary Cochran had, that she is being merchandised, dehumanized into goods for men to buy. The drunken cad Frank Metcalf fails to seduce her. Phillip Grimes makes her feel awkward. After her return to Bidwell, the slick and sleezy New Yorker Alfred Buckley almost obtains her, until he is uncovered as a swindler. Clara's alternative role models frighten her. Aunt Priscilla and Uncle Henderson Woodburn are caricatures of a marriage, not really alive. To Priscilla the world is a place of terror, where wolflike men devour women. She knits stockings for "poor children" but never gives any away. Henderson meanwhile is wrapped up in his account books. The most interesting person Clara meets is Kate Chancellor, a bold and vigorous lesbian socialist, whose manliness and sexual orientation both repel and attract Clara. The image of Kate remains with her for some time, but, as Kate herself knows, she represents too big of a jump for Clara. Anderson himself can entertain Kate as a hypothetical modern possibility but not as a realistic option.

So Clara returns to Bidwell, having passed through experiences but not having really changed much. Her town, we are told, has changed. The corn-cutter is a success. Even the governor comes to town and calls Hugh "one of the greatest intellects and the most useful man that ever lived" (238). The McVey myth is in full bloom. Ed Hall is now a foreman. Ben Peeler, the carpenter, now employs over twenty men and no longer has time for small talk with farmers. Jim Gibson has gained control of Wainsworth's harness shop and plans to bring in cheaper factory-made harnesses to increase profits. In the end he is shot and killed by Wainsworth, an act that within the ethos of the novel seems justifiable homicide. Meanwhile there are "foreigners" about, notably Italians, whom Hugh finds off-putting.

It is to this world, also a world where innuendos of sexual scandals run beneath the surface, that Clara returns from college. Still, like Beaut McGregor, believing in such heroes as Lincoln, Grant, and Sherman, she also is attracted to the successful local hero Hugh. On the other hand, two things undermine his heroic image. First, among some town workers there is a desire to tar and feather Hugh as a cause of their problems. Second, Hugh still sees himself as the "poor white trash" tutored by Sarah Shepard. He believes Clara could not be interested in him. One day, however, he defends her honor and then rides off with her to the county seat to be married. If Hugh is to marry, a reader would probably say, the less flamboyant and dynamic Rose McCoy seems his natural choice, but in a *Winesburg*-like sequence in chapter 12 their relationship miscarries because she is too shy and he too self-conscious.

In a sequence too improbable for any technique but high camp or farce, Clara and Hugh marry. The wedding feast is a miserable drunken binge, leading Clara to complain that her wedding "had aborted into an occasion for the display of ugliness and vulgarity" (296). She recalls her own mother's marriage as a kind of brute submission. Hugh is then unable to perform a sexual act with Clara and in fear flees out the window. Only after Tom Butterworth drags Hugh back to his daughter is the marriage consummated and then only with Clara taking the lead. Clara has been through anger and frustration; Hugh is in "protest against the grotesque position into which he had been thrown by his marriage to Clara" (319). *Poor White* comes to an end with the revolution having finally passed Hugh by, with Hugh no longer useful as an inventor, with Clara the tigress now loving Hugh, "a perplexed boy," and with the still naïve Hugh now questioning the value of the progress of which he has been part.

4

The Short Stories

THE SHORT PROSE FORM—TALE, STORY, SKETCH, ESSAY—WAS ANDERson's forte. His most effective fictional book is a collection of tales and sketches. He plays a very minor role in the history of the American novel, but a more important role in the history of short fiction because of the original nature of some of his best tales and sketches and the unique excellence of his one short-story composite. His books of nonfiction prose include numerous moving, insightful pieces. His autobiographical works are less impressive as wholes than as collections with splendid parts.

After Anderson's early attempts at novels, a kind of epiphany led him into the tales and sketches that became *Winesburg, Ohio.* Prior to that time, although he had written blurbs and articles as an advertising man, his only published story had been "The Rabbit-Pen" (1914), a tale of frustration, desire, and jealousy. Other pieces printed in 1916, besides five stories that went into *Winesburg*, included "Blackfoot's Masterpiece," a sketch of a frustrated artist," and "War," or "The Struggle" as it was then called, a sketch on Polish refugees, later reprinted in *The Triumph of the Egg.*

In 1921 and 1923 Liveright published collections of Anderson's stories, *The Triumph of the Egg* and *Horses and Men*, which include some of his best work. Ten years later in *Death in the Woods* Anderson collected most of his stories from the intervening decade, including two of his very best; and then there were almost a dozen later stories that remained uncollected. All in all there are seven or eight wonderful stories, another seven or eight quite good ones, and an additional handful that can still spark interest. Anderson scholars and critics often focus on the stories since they include much of the writer's best work.[1]

The Triumph of the Egg consists of thirteen tales, the earliest outside of "War" being "Seeds" and "Senility" published in 1918 (drafted in 1917 and 1916), although two taken from the "Mary Cochran" manuscript, "Unlighted Lamps" and "The Door of the Trap," may well be earlier in origination if not publication. The others were written between 1919 and 1921. Some short verses, "The Dumb Man," open the book and set a tone much as "The Book of the Grotesque" does in *Winesburg, Ohio.* Closing the collection is another poem, "The Man with the Trumpet," whose speaker says that those in the room with him "might build temples to themselves" (268–69).[2] The volume's subtitle, "A Book of Impressions from American Life in Tales and Poems," is noteworthy for its emphasis on Anderson's method; and the collection also included "Impressions in Clay," photographs of seven sculptures, based on characters, done by Tennessee Mitchell. *Horses and Men* consists of nine stories. Only "A Chicago Hamlet," a fusion of two stories, one clearly dating from 1916, is of early vintage, although "The Man's Story" draws on ideas from "Talbot Whittingham." "Unused," "An Ohio Pagan," and "Milk Bottles" derive from an unfinished novel, "Ohio Pagans," on which Anderson worked intensively after completing *Poor White.*

The opening tale in both *The Triumph of the Egg* and *Horses and Men* is a first-person narration of an initiation story set in the world of horses and racetracks, to some extent suggesting the influence of Damon Runyan, Ring Lardner, and Mark Twain. In "I Want to Know Why" a youth learns of the basic weakness of mankind. He watches a trainer, whom he deeply admires, at a filthy brothel kissing a prostitute, boasting and swearing. The narrator has difficulty adjusting to this new and disconcerting knowledge about his hero and implicitly about mankind. In "I'm a Fool" an older teenager working as a groom learns of his own weakness. Self-consciously trying to prove he is a man, the youth tells lies about himself to a girl and then realizes, as much as he may like her, that having set up false credentials he cannot ask her out again. At the end he sees himself as a boob. "I Want to Know Why" is generally considered one of Anderson's best stories, certainly of those in the Huck Finn mode. "I'm a Fool," while praised by William Faulkner and Horace Gregory, is more often described as a weak story in which the narrator falls from naïveté into stupidity. It is also, however, a more complex attempt than the straight-line initiation story of "I Want to Know Why," an attempt during which although Anderson may not adequately design the development of his main character but in which he does explore the importance of self-awareness about one's own limitations and confidence in one's actual self.[3]

The other racetrack story in *Horses and Men* is "The Man Who Became a Woman." It is a rich story, one in which the narrator, Herman Dudley, is speaking as a grown man about a time when he was a young swipe and sometime tramp. It revolves around male identity and insecurity, the central episode being a near-rape of the youth by two men in a loft on a rainy night and the youth's subsequent decision to give up his current way of life. It includes some of Anderson's strongest prose and more thoughtful insights than one finds in his novels of the period. In one of the best studies of the short fiction, Rex Burbank shows how ironic indirection, effective use of puzzled narrators, a balanced tone, and controlling symbols lead to successes in stories like "The Man Who Became a Woman" and "I Want to Know Why," and how heavy-handed symbolism and the attempt to use an urbane narrator are frequently at the root of Anderson's failures.[4]

Away from the track but with a comparable technique in *The Triumph of the Egg* is "The Egg," a widely praised tale. The narrator looks back to his youth. The main character is his father, but as in so many Anderson tales the observer, only half understanding what is seen, is as much the subject as the main character is. The father, a cheerful farm worker, and his wife get ambitious to give their boy "something better," and so buy a chicken farm. The farm fails, then they run a restaurant, and then the father makes a pathetic attempt as an entertainer. The most memorable parts are the image of jars with deformed chickens in formaldehyde and the father's futile effort to tell stories and do egg tricks. The story's strength derives from the balance of grotesque exaggeration and pathos. It balances the mood of a fable with social criticism and in miniature achieves that mythopoeic quality that Benjamin Spencer shows is characteristic of Anderson's best work. It is also, as Marc Conner shows, a key transitional text in Anderson's growing reconciliation with the memory of his father.

The Triumph of the Egg was widely praised when it appeared in the fall of 1921 by, among others, H. L. Mencken, Rebecca West, Padraic Colum, and John Peale Bishop. Anderson was at the height of his critical standing at this time. Although he had problems with such novels as "Ohio Pagans" and *Many Marriages*, he wrote some of his best stories between 1919 and 1923. Most of the other tales in *The Triumph of the Egg* deal with lonely figures, failures of communication, or problems with marriages. "Seeds" revolves around an Iowa woman in Chicago badly needing affection and being evicted from her rooming house. She is someone who might be found in Winesburg, and, given her self-imposed psychological blocks, there is no easy solution to her problem.[5] "Unlighted Lamps" is a story of Mary Cochran focusing on her inability to communicate with her father and on his untimely death before they can bridge the gap. "The New Englander" deals with Elsie Leander, a Vermont girl who moves to Iowa to live near an older brother and becomes a frustrated spinster. It is unclear whether the sterility emphasized in the story is the New Englander's, the Midwest village's (despite those ever-present fertile cornfields), or universal. Elsie might well be another Winesburg grotesque.

In "The Door of the Trap" a math teacher at a midwestern college, a bit of a sadist himself, befriends Mary Cochran but sends her off at the end in hopes she will not be just another girl caught in a marriage trap. "The Man in the Brown Coat" is about a historian unable to break through a wall of miscommunication with his wife, the theme being, "Are there no words that lead to life?" "Brothers," which includes a tale within the tale and repeats symbols of enclosure, fog, and compression, tells of an old man who makes up stories about persons in the newspaper being related to him. The interior story concerns a man, perhaps the old man's brother, who murdered his pregnant wife while infatuated with a young secretary, a pattern anticipating *Many Marriages*. In "The Other Woman" a man tells the narrator of making love to a tobacconist's wife, an "earthy" creature, the night before his own wedding. "Motherhood" is a lyrical sketch of a pregnant woman and a young man.

The Triumph of the Egg concludes with a long story, "Out of Nowhere into Nothing." It concerns a young woman, Rosalind Wescott, who six years before had left her small Iowa town for Chicago. Now she returns home to tell her mother she is in love with a married man, Walter Sayers, in Chicago. Although the small town seems dull and sterile, Sayers's suburban environment is just as sterile. Rosalind's mother is one of Anderson's frustrated, bitter, narrow women beaten down by time. Her daughter still seeks "the white wonder of life" (238). This is one of several stories praised by early critics but less appreciated of late. It is one of Anderson's more complex stories, however, and poignantly captures the experience of a young woman caught between two less than desirable options and choosing the one path with some light at the end.

Outside of some experiments with narrative voice and patterns of imagery, the most intriguing aspect of these stories is the role of women. Several have a central female character, in two cases Mary Cochran, or perhaps only one since the teacher is really the main figure in "The Door of the Trap." "Motherhood" is more of a fertility song, to be sure, and "The New Englander" and "Seeds" are about Winesburg-type women. In "Out of Nowhere," however, a young woman much like Helen White, who is never quite developed in *Winesburg*, is at the center and is given a future if not ideal at least as hopeful as that given most of Anderson's male characters. For all of Anderson's deficiencies in portraying women, he did try more than once to explore the potential of talented, insightful women like Mary, Rosalind, and Kit Brandon; and in other books strong women drive much of the action. Around 1930, of course, women, in some of Anderson's nonfiction prose, become his last best hope for America.

HORSES AND MEN

In *Horses and Men* only one story, "Unused," really centers around a woman, and she, May Edgely, is a victim of Bidwell's parochial prejudices. Rarely listed among Anderson's best tales, "Unused" is still a moving story of a capable teenager, the most promising child in a poor family, who gives herself once sexually to a young rogue and finds herself cast as a loose girl. A bizarre double date lands May in a place where she is accosted by town toughs and ends up taking her own life. Anderson was learning that in tales with a potential for maudlin sentimentality the most effective narrator is often the half-understanding observer, in this case played by a man who was then assistant to the doctor who signed May's death certificate, the doctor who provided the epithet "unused" (31) to describe May's life.[6] The assistant provides just the right distance from the events, which also become his own learning experience. This method often served Anderson well, for example in "Death in the Woods."

"Unused" comes by and large from an unfinished manuscript "Ohio Pagans," although in the novel Anderson does not have May die tragically but rather go on to new experiences and frustrations. From the same manuscript also came "An Ohio Pagan," which closes the 1923 collection with the same open-ended hope that "Out of Nowhere into Nothing" and "Departure" provide in *The Triumph of the Egg* and *Winesburg, Ohio*. Set in Bidwell it tells the story of Tom Edwards, an orphan who takes care of a racehorse, works in various jobs, and seeks adventure in his life. Organizationally the story is a bit at loose ends, to be sure, but it seems designed to emphasize tension between romantic adventure and a workaday world of school, work, and gentility. It is also one of Anderson's tales that imbue the natural world with a kind of pastoral mystique.

Outside of the initiation tales, "I'm a Fool" and "The Man Who Became a Woman," the tragedy in "Unused," and the pastoral "An Ohio Pagan," few tales in *Horses and Men* have commanded much interest. "Milk Bottles," originally published as "Why There Must Be a Midwestern Literature," tries too hard to dramatize the difference between serious writing and commercial writing, although it does reflect Anderson's own frustrations and desires. "The Triumph of the Modern, or Send for the Lawyer" is a satire about art, the sincere and the insincere. "The Sad Horn-Blowers" is one of several writings from this period that imply a change in Anderson's perspective on his father. Will Appleton has a cornet-playing father now laid up ill in bed. A man whom Will meets on the train to Erie is also a bad cornet player but provides a tolerant new perspective for Will, who ends the story sadly facing adulthood, rethinking his view of his father, and blowing a horn. On the other hand, "A Chicago Hamlet," which inadequately fuses two separate tales, includes the much earlier story "Broken," in which the main character hates his father and nearly kills him in order to keep his own integrity.

One of Anderson's personal favorites was "The Man's Story," a tale of Edgar Wilson, a romantic poet who runs off to Chicago with a married woman from Kansas. They struggle with poverty, failure, and desire until she is murdered one night. The story revises a piece of "Talbott Whittingham" and, in the eyes of some readers, suggests Anderson's personal guilt over his wives and uncertainty about his achievements. It is not one of his strongest tales, but it is engaging partly because Anderson skillfully employs the observer-narrator, a reporter trying to make sense of Wilson, listening to third-party accounts, and putting the pieces together.

DEATH IN THE WOODS
AND OTHER STORIES

In 1934 Anderson published his final collection of short stories, *Death in the Woods and Other Stories*. The title story is one of his best and most admired; the final story, "Brother Death," while less often taught and studied, is also excellent. The fourteen stories in between include few, outside of "A Meeting South," that have received significant attention. While some are weak, others include passages of strong writing and clever techniques. A few touch on the marriage theme; a few confront nostalgia about the past; some are satiric; but the new element in the fiction of Anderson is a set of sympathetic portrayals of mountain people based on his experiences in rural Virginia after 1927. Such characters, of course, had already appeared in his "nonfiction" writing, for example, *Hello Towns!*

Most of the stories, perhaps eleven, were drafted between 1926 and 1930, with four preceding that time and only "Brother Death," from all available evidence, written afterward. "Death in the Woods" had a long gestation period. The story's basic elements appear in a piece from 1916 that Anderson returned to and expanded and revised several times, once calling it "The Death in the Forest," before publishing the result in 1926 in two versions. He continued to make subtle and significant changes as he prepared it for publication in *Death in the Woods*, particularly to humanize the woman who dies and to enrich the narrator's role.

The story is ostensibly about a young-old woman, less than forty, beaten by life, yet in death again seeming young. She is cruelly treated by her husband and son, after a difficult youth, and then she freezes to death while returning from the country store, stripped of her clothing and groceries by a pack of wolfish dogs. The focus, however, is actually controlled by the narrator, a man recalling the

woman's death from his childhood and making sense of it in different ways over the years. One perspective on the story has always been
that best articulated by Clare Colquitt that the story dehumanizes
the real woman by focusing solely on the boy's perspective and trying to mythify, and mystify, the actual experience.[7] Mary Anne Ferguson, however, although generally critical of Anderson's portrayal
of female characters, sees real growth in the final version of "Death
in the Woods" and more generally in the volume as a whole.[8] To her
the best stories show Anderson moving away from an emphasis only
on a persona seeking meaning in the archetypal toward a shared emphasis on the observer and a reality outside the observer, in this case
the woman. At least since an article by Jon Lawry in 1959, however,
the story has also been seen as crucial to understanding Anderson's
view of the growth of an artist and his recognition that only through
creative artistry can any perceived reality, such as the woman's life
and death, be given a larger meaning for a society and its culture.[9]

Some ambivalence on the part of the reader is elicited from the
start by Anderson's indefiniteness. The woman is old but young. She
"was nothing special. She was one of the nameless ones that hardly
any one knows, but she got into my thoughts" (4).[10] She is generalized as "such an old woman" who is around all small towns and rural
areas. In counterpoint with such generalizations are specific details
about Mrs. Grimes and her hard life, such as also to elicit sympathy
and sadness. At his best, Anderson guides a reader to respond both
to the physical situation being observed and to an observer's wonder
at his own naïve response and fiction-making process. The final passage of the story captures the subtlety and ambivalence of the adult
capturing the youth grasping the meaning of death.

> You see it is likely that, when my brother told the story, that night
> when we got home and my mother and sister sat listening, I did not
> think he got the point. He was too young and so was I. A thing so
> complete has its own beauty.
>
> I shall not try to emphasize the point. I am only explaining why I
> was dissatisfied then and have been ever since. I speak of that only
> that you may understand why I have been impelled to try to tell the
> simple story over again. (24)

The boy, of course, had heard it all at secondhand from his
brother but even then knew the brother had not understood, and

ever since the boy has tried and tried to understand better, even as the speaker in Walt Whitman's "Out of the Cradle Endlessly Rocking" continues to reconceptualize, as man and poet, his younger self's first acquaintance with death.

"Brother Death," which closes the book, despite the title is a very different story, although both stories exist in that mythopoetic half-world between fable and realism. It uses a more conventional authorial narrator. While one character, young Ted, is dying, throughout the story the death more poignantly indicated by the title is the death of the soul that results from the need for the successful man to dominate his environment and other people. Little Ted and his loving sister, Mary, may remind readers of Paul and Florence Dombey suffering in *Dombey and Son* before their autocratic father, who is to be sure drawn more grotesquely by Dickens than is John Grey by Anderson. Perhaps because Grey's significant physical action in the story is only cutting down, against the wishes of wife and children, two stately oaks, not treating his family in beastly ways, he is not literally as repulsive a character as Dombey. He exerts masculine power by cutting down the oaks, thereby also striking out at his wife's family, whom he replaced on the land, and rejecting the attempt of his son Don to dissuade him. Don, so much like him in their conflict, will experience the same death for, as John says, "Something in you must die before you can possess and command" (297). While Ted dies of his illness, he "would never have to face the more subtle and terrible death that had come to his older brother" (298).

The story is one of Anderson's tales of Virginia country people, but also emblematic of a theme developing in his work for years, the sterility of a world whose primary values are success, control, and power over others. Anderson does not repeat here what he had covered elsewhere, mechanization of people's lives, standardization, boredom, loss of purpose. It may not be a coincidence that John has the same last name as Fred Grey, the successful industrialist of *Dark Laughter*, whose wife finds him so incapable of love. "Brother Death," however, emphasizes the effect of such drives on the one with power. In line with Anderson's exploration at this time of female potential as an alternative to failed American manhood, moreover, the theme is gendered: not only is Mary a counter to the very masculine father and older brother, but also she and Ted have a very significant and sexually suggestive discussion of whether women as well as men might have limbs amputated, as the two trees were cut off.

These are the two best stories, but a few others are still engaging. "A Meeting South" gets attention mostly for the character David, a young, lame, romantic, alcoholic, southern poet, based on William Faulkner. It draws on some of Anderson's early tall tale material and, drafted in 1924 and first published in 1925, is also of a piece with the New Orleans parts of *Dark Laughter*. "That Sophistication" is a satire of artsy expatriate pretenders and phoniness. "The Lost Novel" addresses the problem of a writer who publishes one fine book but cannot get another finished and in his frustration and obsession treats his family cruelly, its pathos conveying Anderson's self-irony and his preoccupation with the connections among gender, authority, and artistry.

Two marriage tales are light and humorous, "Why They Got Married" and "There She Is—She Is Taking Her Bath" (first drafted in 1922), a skillful jeu d'esprit of a perhaps cuckold, jealous and confused about his wife's perhaps adultery. "The Flood" is a later and more serious story of a widowed professor writing a book on values but able to find new love with his wife's sister at the end, a conclusion, however, that is at best ambivalent as to whether that new relationship is a good thing. "In a Strange Town" also concerns a professor, who leaves his home, as Anderson more than once had, to find himself anew. It is self-indulgent but movingly traces the professor's reactions to the death of a student and his groping for its meaning. "The Return" is an earlier tale of a man finding he cannot go home again to his old town. "The Fight" is generally seen merely as a piece reflecting the tension between Anderson and Ernest Hemingway, but it actually deals effectively with the immature adult male unable to outgrow petty frustrations of his youth.

Some of the engaging tales are those of hill people. "Another Wife" concerns a widowed physician who moves to Virginia and falls for a woman there, but at the end is unsure whether his decision to marry her is wise. Anderson is often good at portraying uncertainty, vacillation, and ambivalence in relationships. "Like a Queen" is of a piece with Anderson's essays on women as the last best hope of America. First titled "Beauty," then "Alice," and only later "Like a Queen," it tells the story of a Tennessee singer who turned to drink and gambling and by the time the narrator met her was middle-aged and dumpy but still exuded a regal nature, a beauty that entrances the naïve narrator, who mystifies "the female" as Anderson had "the Negro" in *Dark Laughter*. "These Mountaineers" tells of the narrator getting lost while on a fishing expedition and being invited into the home of a mountaineer. His daughter, a "hell cat," is thin and wild-looking. When at a later time the narrator tries to give her money, she being pregnant by a rather nasty youth, she proudly rejects the gift. Anderson depicts mountaineer pride as another positive standard against a decadent, sterile, conforming industrial civilization, but he does not so vaguely mystify it as he does "the Negro" or "the Female."

"A Jury Case" deals with a group of moonshiners, mean mountain men capable of betraying their neighbor to save their own skin. Harvey Groves, Cal Long, and George Small, a sniveling coward, buy a still. Harvey runs off with it. Cal prods George into killing Harvey and then runs off, leaving George alone to face a jury. Anderson complicates the narrative by having one Luther Ford, a local, tell the story to an outside narrator, increasing both distance and credibility, to be sure, but making the conclusion awkward and the implications unclear. Finally, "A Sentimental Journey" also uses the double, or triple, narrator, the authorial figure hearing from his friend David about Joe, a fierce-looking moonshiner who himself told David his story. Joe and his son had once left the hills to work in a mine but, despite higher pay checks, soon returned to the mountain home they missed. The most striking scene is one of Joe and his son on a freezing day forcing their way into someone's home to warm themselves at the fire.

LATER STORIES

There are a dozen or so other stories that Anderson either published or left in manuscript form.[11] The two best sources for them are *Certain Things Last: The Selected Short Stories of Sherwood Anderson*, edited by Charles E. Modlin and *The Sherwood Anderson Reader*, edited by Paul Rosenfeld. Modlin indicates that in a few instances Rosenfeld tinkered too much with Anderson's manuscripts. Most of these tales come from 1934 or afterward. None are among the author's very best. They range over some of the same topics as earlier tales albeit at times from a more mature perspective as in the case of marriage or family stories such as "Mrs. Wife," "The Yellow Gown," the more grotesque "Nobody Laughed," and "Daughters," a tale about a father unable to handle his two daughters. "The Corn Planting" is a fine tale about parents losing a son. While the parents are seen rather indirectly through a double narrative screen, the outside narrator and a high school principal who knows the family well, the story is, as Marc Conner suggests, a kind of final coda to Anderson's long grappling with father-son issues. Here the son, however, dies and the father, and mother, albeit perhaps in a daze, return to the firm and lasting and stable reality of planting corn that will grow and live.

All in all the short story accomplishment is impressive. Anderson drew on techniques of George Borrow, Turgenev, and Chekhov rather than the plotted stories of Maupassant and O. Henry or the social fictions of James and Wharton. His contribution lies in a kind of impressionistic portrayal of an inner tension. In a few cases his characters are really grotesques. They are more often lonely, baffled, exiled, or mistreated by their communities. Relationships are not Anderson's forte, thus one reason his long narratives do not succeed. Insight, momentary, into a character's bafflement or narrowness or alienation is his strength. His best tales are sketches or portrayals of imperfect attempts at understanding a world of wonder.[12]

5
Novels of Midlife Crisis

MANY MARRIAGES

Two of Anderson's three collections of stories appeared within a short period after the publication of *Poor White*, 1921 and 1923, and they include some of his best. Such successes did elevate Anderson, in the eyes of numerous critics, into the top rank of American writers. Wharton and Cather may have been stronger talents, but at the time were more likely to be dubbed "best female novelists." Dreiser was a looming figure, but had not published a novel since *The Genius* in 1915, and that was hardly a success. Sinclair Lewis's early work received little attention, but with *Main Street* (1920) and *Babbitt* (1922) Lewis was labeled, along with Anderson, as a bright new talent, ironic given Anderson's disdain for his fellow midwesterner. James Branch Cabell and Ellen Glasgow were distinctly "southern" to a northern press, and Fitzgerald was still only a potential new talent "this side of paradise." The literary, or rather the prose, landscape was transitional enough for Anderson temporarily to be placed near the top.

This standing did not last long. Anderson did not publish another highly regarded book, although *A Story-Teller's Story* was undervalued, some of the later stories are excellent, some of the nonfiction quite good, and *Dark Laughter* sold relatively well. He continued to publish prolifically, both fiction and nonfiction, but most of his collections received limited attention and from then on he remained in the position of significant minor writer.

Anderson's next two novels are embarrassing at times, even though one was his best seller and the other apparently his personal favorite.

For the first time he focuses on middle-aged or at least long-married men, not young people. Both novels, while romantic efforts to define a liberated approach to life, are also self-indulgent laments of a man's married state. Each makes a limited attempt at self-irony, at criticism of the protagonist, who in both cases is really quite foolish, but the irony is awkward. Gertrude Stein's influence on Anderson was healthy; D. H. Lawrence's was not. *Many Marriages* is by someone too infatuated with *The Rainbow* and *Women in Love* as it appeals for sensuality and liberation from the constraints of bureaucracy, everydayness, marriage, commercialism, and conventions. In 1921 Anderson specifically praised *Women in Love*. In *Many Marriages* he romanticizes and mystifies the exotic, the "Negro," the sensual. Like other books of the 1920s it blames what is wrong with America on "Puritanism," a Puritanism closer to Victorian gentility than to anything in the world of John Winthrop or Cotton Mather. Whatever its weaknesses, Anderson felt that he had effectively shown "the process of thought and the effect of thought on unexpressed lives."[2] In 1922 he wrote Huebsch, "If it comes off . . . it will be the biggest, most sustained and moving thing I've done."[3] Years later he wrote to artist Georgia O'Keeffe that *Many Marriages* was a book designed to bring "flesh into prose" and to Italian publisher Ulrico Hoepli that it was still his personal favorite of the novels.[4]

Anderson began work on *Many Marriages* in 1920 and 1921, a period when his marriage to Tennessee was falling apart, when he was moving around between Alabama and Chicago and New Orleans, when he was taking up painting more seriously and actually having shows in Chicago and New York, and when he was seeking to do a new kind of fiction. It was a period when he wrote stories with a negative slant on marriage such as "The Other Woman," "The Door of the Trap," "Brothers," and "Out of Nowhere into Nothing." Other stories of the period are of characters with doubts about their manhood, "Broken," "The Man Who Became a Woman," and "The Man's Story." John Webster in *Many Marriages* is Anderson's most fully developed character with doubts about his manhood and his marriage.

Webster at thirty-eight is a prosperous washing machine manufacturer in a Wisconsin town, as Anderson again diversifies his midwestern settings. A quiet and slightly graying man, he comes to feel he crushed his dreams in order to succeed as a businessman: "The whole structure of business . . . was an odd affair" (8), foreign to him, who had not wanted it but inherited it.[5] What those dreams may have been is never clear, but John now senses a feeling of rebirth, a strange quasi-religious experience as if he "had suddenly begun walking in a new world" (6). All this may merely signify, as Anderson notes twice in the book, that John is sexually attracted to a younger woman, his secretary, and is bored with his wife of eighteen years. The foreword is an invitation to read the novel in a radical way. It posits a person desiring to leave home and spouse but unable to cross that threshold as he is sucked "down and down into a bottomless pit."[6] About the wife, Mary, we are told very little. More than any other of Anderson's significant characters she is dehumanized. From the first she is described as one whose "face is a blank thing" (21) that has no life in it. She is the "Puritan in full flower" (64) opposed to any sexual fulfillment not tied to bearing children. She is never given speech and almost never described. Other than the pathetic image of her in John's room during the book's central scene, a reader has only the story of John years before coming upon her nude sleeping body in a friend's home. Overwhelmed by the experience, he runs home in the cold, then returns to ask Mary to be his wife. At that moment Mary is a radiant "jewel" of "regal grace," the "Virgin" he momentarily worships (126). Later John comes to feel that he was fooled and trapped in that "wedding moment," just as he was trapped in business by his inheritance. The inert wife living in their house has little to do with the "girl he married"; she is not the same person (193). The only insight provided into Mary is from a scene occurring not long before the "nude" scene; she remembers seeing a man, also naked, in a field beside a slow train on which she was riding. In her imagination she had later mistaken John for that man in the field. Therefore, one infers, both partners have been trapped into this marriage, although what the man in the field would have meant to Mary no one knows. In fact, the expected pattern for John's vision of Mary might well be a clothed figure whose garments are a false sign of her character in contrast with the "real" nude self in the field that Mary is never able to engage. Instead Anderson opts for the vulnerable young self to whom John, in a mistaken humanitarian moment, is drawn. The whole book grows out of Anderson's second failed marriage, and while there is no direct connection between Tennessee and Mary, and certainly no similarity between Elizabeth Prall and Natalie Swartz, there seem to be close ties between John's sense of failure, of being on the wrong road, of searching, and the self-exploration of Anderson himself in a very autobiographical period of his life, a stretch with these two novels plus at least three other books that are deliberately autobiographical in design.

Jane, the seventeen-year-old daughter, also says little. John intends to give her a new philosophy of life with respect for the flesh and sensuality, but it is not clear how she fits into his vision. The other young woman, Natalie Swartz, has a clearer role to play. Daughter of a drunken Irish saloon keeper, Natalie carries clear class markers that allow John to assume sexual freedoms with her. Prior to attaching himself to her, John has been going to Chicago to see prostitutes, carrying in his mind the common dichotomy of a fantasy for the ideal woman and lust for the whore. Natalie as his own possession provides him with a new model; she "opens him up" (66) as part of his rebirth, but in her own mother's words she is "you husky whore" (255). Off John goes with her as the story closes, to what end is unclear. The philosophy of rebellion has given way to the actuality of a new relationship in which the male is, by virtue of his social class, the superior and in charge but hardly a positive Lawrentian hero.

A dominant metaphor throughout the book is the house—houses to live in, to look through, to be. John's house, he feels, has been vacant twenty years. He asks why people cannot "be," as they live in, many houses over the years. As a plea for free love, the narrator asks whether entering bodies cannot be like entering houses, one day to be done more freely (15): people must not "lock the doors of their being" (69). Another motif of sensuality running through *Many Marriages* is "the Negro," a theme more fully developed in *Dark Laughter* and found in the mid-twenties in writings of other authors such as Carl Van Vechten, Dubose Heyward, and William Faulkner. John thinks of "black men at work in the forest of the world of his imagination" (14), and naked in his own room he sings a "negro song" (23). The African American symbolizes for John a preindustrial, unified, sensual world, in contrast to his current life, his wife, his business, and the conventions of everyday urban life.

The central scene of *Many Marriages*, covering half the book albeit with enclosed flashbacks, is a bizarre Lawrentian ritual in John's bedroom. Purchasing votive candles and other ceremonial trappings at a Catholic goods store and taking a preparatory walk in the woods to renew the "animal life" in him (84), John indulges in a "purification ceremony" in his room, dancing nude as his wife and daughter are made to look on. He then embarks on a confessional narrative to Jane, as if he were a dramatist staging the drama of his own conversion (153). Within his paean to a life of the senses are enfolded the narrative of his coming upon the nude sleeping Mary and their subsequent marriage, Mary's own memory of the naked man in the field, and a few of Jane's thoughts. Mary otherwise is described as an "old boat," something that had gone on for years without living, one who keeps an iron lid tightly on a well of unexpressed thought (164). In John's mind she is like the repressed world of commerce. Jane's reaction is to gush out to her father, "I don't care what's happened. I love you" (145). Confused, lonely, and clearly not in sympathy with her mother, despite fearing her suicide, Jane still senses a new spirit of life in her self: "I'm a great little swimmer in seas" (202).

Whatever the irony directed at John, and despite the awkward authorial admission that all of this was just a ruse to dump a boring wife and run off with a younger woman (256), *Many Marriages* dehumanizes Mary as brutally as John does. Despite Anderson's confusion about gender roles, this characterization is still singular in his writing. Little in the book justifies John's disdain except what he himself states. Mary herself is denied a voice, and the colorless daughter, Jane, has no sympathy for her mother. To top it off, the housekeeper, Katherine, for some reason, has never liked Mrs. Webster and also decides to leave. Mary in effect has been but a symbol for all that John rejects about middle-class life, and so near the end when she really is dead there is little over which to grieve. John meanwhile finds Natalie waiting for him. Off they go with the swagger of a "sailor" and an "actress," of course to no very clear future. While Anderson leaves no doubt that one should not be particularly optimistic about John's future, he also leaves no reason to regret the loss of what has been rejected. The picture of marriage, indeed of "many marriages," is one of total selfishness with no sensitivity to the needs or character of the "other," no sense of the other as having a voice and being a person of equal value. Mary has little in common with Anderson's own first two wives, but the author does seem to have been working through in this novel some problems from those earlier experiences even as he was not far from his third marriage, to Elizabeth Prall. He was not, moreover, through with these themes, which continue in *Dark Laughter.*

DARK LAUGHTER

Dark Laughter is Anderson's second exploration of the midlife crisis of an unhappily married man. In a sense it is a sequel to *Many Marriages* picking up after the husband has fled and asking, what next? Bruce Dudley in the end is only marginally more sympathetic than John Webster, but unlike *Many Marriages* this novel also has a somewhat sympathetic female character. Dudley actually becomes the "other man" in a flirtation with that unhappily married woman, Aline Grey. When she leaves her husband and child, there remains for her, however, the question, "What next?"

In *Dark Laughter* Anderson uses the African American to symbolize a healthy norm set against an increasingly standardized, industrialized, conformist white middle class. In doing so he falls into some now embarrassing racist assumptions and descriptions; and he never develops a black character as a significant individual or even as an independent voice. The Negroes, or "niggers" as the phrasing usually runs, are rather a chorus and a contextual backdrop against which the plot lines develop. In a letter to Babs Finley in 1920 he had written, "I wonder why I seem to understand and love the niggers most."[7] The same year he wrote to Jerome Blum, "I am going after the American nigger. He's got something lovely that's never been touched."[8]

As in other novels Anderson extends the story of his protagonist, in this case Dudley, up to a certain point and then moves on to the story of a second main character, in this case Aline Grey, developed in a different setting. The stories do intersect, and occasionally the story lines enrich and reinforce each other. *Dark Laughter* sold better than Anderson's other novels, and it also allowed him to work through the marriage theme, as earlier books had allowed him to work through the young-man-develops theme.

Bruce Dudley is really John Stockton, who deserted his wife in Chicago, grew a beard, changed his name, and now labors in an Indiana factory on the Ohio River, coincidentally in his old hometown. Such flights from adult responsibility have in literature often suggested immaturity and retreat to childhood even when also intended as a rejection of conformity and a statement of freedom. Mark Twain and Huckleberry Finn remained important for Anderson. The river, in this case the Ohio-Mississippi system from Indiana to New Orleans, is a motif throughout the novel. For Anderson it represents the lost youth of America (15, 17), the vitality of a Midwest before the railroad and factories killed the laughter and music.[9] For Dudley it calls up memories of his childhood, his mother, and a boat trip the family took to Louisville, when his mother and an unnamed young man had an unspoken but significant communication between them. It also suggests the beginning of a great Walt Whitman–like American poetry that is being lost. Perhaps, the narrator muses, "getting on" successfully in modern industry has cost the white man the vitality and naturalness of the river, the pioneers, and the "Negro," who, however, to be sure, has not been allowed to be "getting on."

Dark Laughter and *Many Marriages* are the two Anderson works with a distinctly primitivist bent, the earlier novel reflecting his reading of D. H. Lawrence and the latter showing some influence of his friend Jean Toomer.[10] The impressionistic lyricism that works so well in Toomer's *Cane*, where the world of black Americans in the South and in Washington comes alive in a powerfully suggestive way, is not effective in Anderson's prose. It seems affected, derivative, and there only for special effects. Toomer's primitive portraits suggest real people, but in *Dark Laughter* people of color are generalized—singing, laughing, dancing, knowingly mocking the ways of white folks but never discernible as people. The motif was useful to Anderson not because of a deep interest in racial issues but as one way to attack modern standardization and mechanization, and to lament the loss of vitality and value placed on the individual. The tenth chapter of the novel takes Bruce to New Orleans for five months and is an impressionistic lyrical hymn dominated by images of the African American and summer heat. It comes between chapters on Bruce's marriage to Bernice and scenes with Sponge Martin and his wife in Old Harbor. "New Orleans is not Chicago. It isn't Cleveland or Detroit. Thank God for that!" (76). New Orleans becomes a thematic pole, set first against Chicago and later Paris.[11]

Anderson frequently portrayed marriages and professions as ties from which to be freed. There are few happy marriages or settled professional commitments in his novels and stories. One of the better adjusted couples is in this novel, Sponge Martin and his wife. Sponge is a wiry, uninhibited, tobacco-chewing, hard-drinking worker with a craftsman's skill and the effrontery to tell off his boss. The wife is tough and lusty, and this working-class pair is the only sign of real vitality in the book other than "the Negro."

Bruce, however, cannot be Sponge. He is too much the dreamer, too self-conscious, too clumsy at manual labor. Bruce was a journalist, his wife, Aline, the more sophisticated writer. Bruce resented his wife's success and her camaraderie with the literati of Chicago. He would gladly have put her on a pedestal but could not abide her smug pretensions and artsy talk. In an intriguing reversal Anderson has Bruce call Bernice a man-hater and says her male characters are all weak. Anderson may even have in mind Poe's "Berenice" with its theme of castration.

What the sequence tellingly reflects is Anderson's ambivalence about art and literature. He values the bardic role the writer can play and the craft a writer develops; but in a strong American tradition he disdains art as an institution, what he would call "phony aestheticism," and the hold of literary conventions on an author. He was a romantic in feeling that he needed to break from conventions to get at a new reality, in seeking the "real" in internal experiences, in valuing the "individual" so highly, and in turning—during and after his period with initiation stories and flights from wedlock—more and more to an anti-industrial or preindustrial, antiurban perspective on his world. The true writer to Bruce is not Bernice but Tom Wills, the city desk editor, whose literary ambitions derive from his response to real life not art talk. Although Bruce is not Anderson, neither is this perspective presented ironically, and Anderson often saw himself in the same terms, moving from a quasi-journalistic refraction of reality into the more impressionistic mode that captured a meaningful inner experience.

In the middle of *Dark Laughter* Bruce drops out for eighty pages while the story of Aline Grey develops. The method is similar to that in *Poor White*, where Hugh McVey drops out while the story of Clara Butterworth advances. In *Dark Laughter*, to be sure, the stories are of failed marriages not ambitious youth. Aline, wife of a successful industrialist Fred Grey, resents being taken for granted, being put on a pedestal, and being bored in Old Harbor. Bruce catches her eye, and when she needs a new gardener he is available and then becomes her lover. While the affair disrupts her marriage, it is not clear that her departure promises any more happy of a future for her than did Bruce's from Bernice for him or John Webster's from Mary for him.

Beneath the sense of frustration running through *Dark Laughter* lies the Great War. Aline met Fred in Paris after the war, a war that took the lives of her brother and her fiancé, a war based on lies (179)—men lying, women lying, priests lying—a war based on false ideas and corrupt behavior. Aline had gone to Europe with Esther and Joe Walker, "modern" types but also rotten people, schemers who would corrupt Aline. At one point Esther makes a lesbian overture to Aline and in time comes to have contempt for her naïve midwestern friend. The "Walker crowd" are regulars at parties such as the one at Rose Frank's apartment, characterized by sophisticated arty talk, cigarette smoke, and sexual looseness (twenty-nine ways of love-making?), or the Quat'z Arts Ball of Paris. Anderson is ambivalent about Paris.[12] While it smacks of decadent aestheticism and postwar excess, it also exudes a vitality not unlike that of the black population in New Orleans. For the purposes of *Dark Laughter*, however, it is the Rose Frank and Esther Walker world that drives Aline into the arms of Fred Grey, a young American from a good eastern college with a rich father and a more wholesome outlook on life. Aline actually did favor another, unnamed man in Rose's apartment, in a scene recalling Bruce's mother's brief romantic view of an unnamed man on a riverboat. The man, however, disappears and Fred is the remaining alternative. Out of reaction, fear, or desire for security she agrees to marry him. They cling to each other (174) and marry, even though that one hour may have been the only time they felt attracted to each other, as John Webster had only the one misleading epiphany with Mary that led to their unhappy marriage. Aline was a "nice" girl, whereas Paris women were "ugly," morally speaking. She was an American girl, sweet and fine, who should not even have been participating in Parisian vulgarities (195). After the wedding, however, a wall develops between Fred and Aline as she realizes he is a jerk; as his business consumes his life completely, only in part driven by guilt over being in Europe when his father, the owner, died; as she does not rest easily on the pedestal assigned her; and as she fancies herself a "stone woman" or a "nun," but in any case un-fulfilled.

Fred is angrier at the lover in the garden as a threat to his control than as a rival for Aline's passion. Successful in business, Fred would still prefer to be surrounded by a wall safely shutting out the Other. His interior monologue in Chapter 35 reflects his fear of Aline, of being left alone, of having his world threatened, of having a wife whose child is not his. It is the one section of the book in which Fred is the main character, as Bernice momentarily in Chapter 5 had been. The deserted spouse, he does not die like Mary Webster, but neither does he face his single future confidently as we infer Bernice does, or as perhaps Cornelia Anderson once did.

Bruce and Aline, meanwhile, are hardly facing a promising fu-ture. Bruce may be in love (222) and feel for the first time that he can center his life outside himself and that he is slowly "building his house" (231). He also, however, believes marriage is a relic of bar-barism, a hypothesis unfortunately buttressed by the comment that Negro men and women, his image of positive vitality in the novel, just "take up" and don't bother about marrying. Rejecting the tradi-tional ending of the romantic novel, marriage, Anderson concludes two novels of this period with open-ended but unpromising adulter-ous relationships, no more likely to last than the marriages they re-place. The two books ending with husband and wife together, *Poor White* and *Windy McPherson's Son*, present such bizarre situations that they hardly validate marriage. Harder to find in the endings of *Many Marriages* and *Dark Laughter*, however, are signs of irony or indica-tions of just how ironically one is to view the couples going off to-gether. Today it is hard not to laugh at the pretenses of the couples, but although Anderson can be critical of Bruce Dudley and John Webster, he also seems sympathetic to their desire to break free from stifling wedlock. Notable, however, is the voice he does give to Aline and even to Bernice after the stifling portrayal of Mary Webster. From Mary Cochran to Kit Brandon, Anderson often tried to portray the independent woman, and he may have succeeded best in his very last attempt when he presented her as seen through the eyes of a somewhat puzzled middle-aged male. Otherwise he never quite fig-ured her out. In *Dark Laughter* at least he dramatizes male and fe-male both escaping unhappy marriages, and with that ending he had worked through some critical themes of mid-career.

"OHIO PAGANS"
AND "FATHER ABRAHAM"

Two other manuscripts that Anderson was unable to complete before writing *Many Marriages* shed additional light on his mid-career
concerns. One, the shorter, is a work he wanted to do on Abraham
Lincoln, like Twain and Whitman a nineteenth-century American he
particularly admired. After an opening epigraph from Stephen A.
Douglas emphasizing in 1861 Lincoln's ingenuousness, Anderson
zeroes in on the two traits that most interest him, Lincoln's amazing
storytelling ability, Rabelaisian in its richness, and his profound
worry and concern for other human beings and related ability to appreciate experiences from the Other's perspectives. "Father Abraham" develops around a criminal case in the Midwest. A German
farmer is being tried for the rape of a fourteen-year-old girl who
works for the farmer and his wife, the girl having severely injured
her back in a fall during the episode. Although conviction seems certain, the narrator implies that Abe's uncanny ability to appreciate
the event from the perspective of each one of the three principals,
including the wife's devastation at being left without her breadwin-
ner, will lead either to some appeal of the decision or to some
growth in Lincoln himself. The epiphany Abe experiences, however,
is a connection between the case and the death of Ann Rutledge, his
one true love. The manuscript then moves on to a contrast between
on the one hand the true love of Ann and Abe and on the other the
career-oriented but loveless marriage of Abe and Mary Todd. Soon
the manuscript fizzles out with nowhere to go on either front, but
with Mary Todd Lincoln not coming out much better than had Mary
Webster in *Many Marriages*.[13]

The other manuscript, "Ohio Pagans," is the novel Anderson
started after completing *Poor White*.[14] It tells the story of May Edgely
of Bidwell, Ohio, and is Anderson's first attempt at a novel with a female protagonist since Mary Cochran. May's family are pariahs in
town, both older sisters having gone "on the turf" long ago and
three brothers being merely tough punks. May is the great hope of
the family, a top student in school and unblemished morally. Then
one Jerome Hadley seduces her while berry picking and she soon
loses her reputation. She does find a new friend, Maud from Fort
Wayne, although Maud's father has forbidden contact with any of

the Edgelys. Even living on the same street, he says, is "like living in the midst of niggers." With much more detail, the narrative is close to that of "Unused" through the dance at the "Dewdrop" on Sandusky Bay, where Maud and May are connecting with two much older men, one a grocer sweet on Maud. In "Unused," as mentioned in Chapter 4, May, recognized by some Bidwell boys, ends up drowning in the bay, a tragic victim and a wasted potential.

In the novel May goes out to the beach with one of the Bidwell youths, Sid Gould, but turns on him, hits him over the head with a piece of driftwood, and flees. The next part of the manuscript picks her up four years later with May having spent the last three years as nurse and teacher to a child of a Mr. and Mrs. Overmyer. With a new identity, May Howard of Fort Wayne, she has rebuilt her "tower of romance," picking up a motif from earlier in the novel. One earlier sequence connecting Mary and her father related an episode, somewhere between dream and reality, of a prince fleeing a marriage forced on him by his father and being chased by a huge black man working for his father. May ends up nursing the prince in his illness, or dreaming the same—it is not clear for there is no follow-up except that the "tower of romance" continues as a motif. One might also detect a parallel between on the one hand Abe Lincoln, Ann Rutledge, and Mary Todd, and on the other the prince, May, and his career-based fiancée.

Also working for the Overmyers, where May is nurse and tutor, is Tom Edwards, the stable man and protagonist of the published short story "An Ohio Pagan." Tom, too, is an innocent, who grew up in Clyde we are told and fled town when as a boy he learned he had to attend school instead of working with horses. At the Overmyers' now he becomes the object of a flirtation by Mrs. Kate Overmyer, and Anderson backs up to provide, as is his wont, a good bit of Kate's story too. Meanwhile May has taken a fancy to Tom, though it should be added that now and then she also remembers romantically her seducer, Jerome Hadley. At one point, most likely in a fit of jealousy, she screams out on the steps that Kate is trying to seduce Tom. Then, of course, she must leave the house.

The final parts of the manuscript, or really typescript (overall there are around 250 completed pages of type) revolve mostly around Tom, now working as an ice cutter, and his two friends, Elmer and Will, who hate each other. Will is a small fat hedonist, resenting his parents' fat genes, but showing a good bit of taste for literature and European culture. Elmer is a labor agitator and idealist, who gave up a girlfriend, whom he remembers fondly, to follow his political ideals. The mutual contempt between Elmer and Will, both of whose stories the narrator takes time to trace, culminates in Elmer's drowning in the bay one winter day while they are fighting.

Meanwhile May has been hired as a caretaker for an elderly couple, Ebenezer Stout and his wife. One day she sees Tom, now working in a machine shop, and in the final scene at the door of the Stout home, where he has walked with her, she does not invite him in. If the final sentences imply anything, it is that despite her attraction to him and his desire for her, she will not trust men again or have an entangling alliance. Implicitly, it seems, she will spend her life nursing a series of Ebenezer Stouts. Although Anderson never published "Ohio Pagans," he was also not willing to conclude it with what might have been a quite reasonable union of two romantic and much wounded people. Marriage is never the comic resolution of a Sherwood Anderson fiction.

6

The Nonfiction

ANDERSON'S PRIMARY GENRES UNTIL THE MID-TWENTIES WERE THE novel and the tale. He published eight books of prose fiction by 1925 and other manuscripts of novels lay unpublished or incomplete. There was also one collection of verse and, in 1924, his "autobiography" appeared. From then on Anderson published only four more books of prose fiction—two novels, *Tar*, and a set of tales; one more book of verse; a set of plays; but counting the posthumously published *Memoirs* seven books of nonfiction. The autobiographies include some of his best writing, and some of the essays wear better than do most of the novels.

A Story-Teller's Story came out in 1924. *Tar: A Midwest Childhood*, an autobiographical fiction of Anderson's youth, appeared in 1926. In his final years Anderson was composing his memoirs, a more straightforward account of his life, that appeared posthumously as edited by Paul Rosenfeld. An authoritative edition was finally published in 1969, edited by Ray White. In other prose of 1926 to 1940 Anderson tested a series of themes, perspectives, and voices to explore America critically but affectionately. Moving beyond his Carl Van Vechten–like use of the African American as healthy primitive set against decadent industrialized bureaucratic America, he considered women, southern farmers, and mountaineers as new models for the vitality sapped by so much of modern life. Anderson's friendship and then marriage with Eleanor engaged him more directly in reform causes, and in the 1930s like other writers he took up with the American Writers' Congress and adopted a generally leftist perspective. As with his hero, Dreiser, however, it would be a mistake to define Anderson's politics in categorical terms. Unions and parties could, for him, defeat the individual and his healthy vitality as surely as business and government could. He sympathized with the oppressed and he could identify what he did not like, but as had been true from his first book he had more trouble describing what he would like.

In some ways Anderson's experiments with voice and style in nonfiction are as revealing as his themes are. Outside of the autobiographies, the nonfiction includes two collections of varied essays, *Sherwood Anderson's Notebook* (1926) and *No Swank* (1934), which do have recurring motifs, and the three more focused collections, *Hello Towns!* (1929), *Perhaps Women* (1931), and *Puzzled America* (1935). Like the *Memoirs*, then, the short work *Home Town* (1940) provides a fitting capstone to the last part of Anderson's career.

Sherwood Anderson's Notebook was published by Liveright in 1926, two years after *A Story-Teller's Story*, one year after *Dark Laughter* and the same year as *Tar.* It includes material, on Anderson's life and on other writers, dating back to 1916, but most of the text was written in 1924 and 1925. The glue connecting the various essays and reflections is a quintet of interspersed musings called "Notes out of a Man's Life," which, along with an opening passage called "From Chicago," provide a quasi-autobiographical outline to the book and connect it to *A Story-Teller's Story* and *Tar.*

One theme is asserted in the foreword, a letter to Horace Liveright, complaining of the "mess of cheapness into which the modern world has got" (17) and blaming not only the public for lowered tastes of the day but also writers and publishers.[1] Drawing on ideas adopted from Gertrude Stein, Anderson's *Seven Arts* friends, and others, Anderson sought in the *Notebook* a new form, albeit a pastiche, as he had sought a new kind of autobiography in *A Story-Teller's Story* and a new kind of fiction in *Winesburg, Ohio.* The nonautobiographical essays, largely revised material from the past decade, posit a set of aesthetic values and also attack standardization, cheapness, and what he feared was an increasing quiet desperation in America. Taken as a whole, along with the autobiographical "Notes," they provide the most extensive aesthetic statement made by Anderson, and can be read in conjunction with *The Modern Writer* (1925), a lecture-essay tying the modernist movement to a defense by serious writers against the excesses of industrialization and standardization.[2]

The second section, "Four American Impressions" (1919), includes earlier pieces praising Stein for opening up the English language in new ways; Ring Lardner, who, he says, like Mark Twain put
a new reality into stories; and Paul Rosenfeld, friend and critic as
role model; and criticizing Sinclair Lewis, to Anderson a writer of
humorless dreariness. Also in the book are essays on George Bellows
and Alfred Stieglitz, two positive models from the world of visual
arts, loving life and craft and in Stieglitz's case serving as a telling
contrast to Henry Ford, who set out to make a factory-centered
America standardized and ugly.

A pivotal essay is "A Note on Realism" (1924), in which Anderson
separates himself from an aesthetic of replicating or mirroring reality, which has to him little value because art is, simply put, not reality
but, one might say, a refraction of reality. Anderson's artist must feed
on reality or he will starve, and the writer must use what he knows
best. It is, however, the imaginative truth that counts; what the writer
does with his material separates good art from good journalism.
Today this argument might belabor the obvious, but at a time
when—albeit in the midst of impressionism, expressionism, Dada,
futurism, and other "nonrealistic" movements—serious writers were
arguing for the need to face reality directly, it was significant for one
of the, even if misnamed, "new realists" to assert a distinction between serious literature that shapes a new perspective on reality and
appearances that make up what is generally called the real.

An earlier essay, "An Apology for Crudity" (1916), appears late in
the volume and justifies the radical vernacular and vitality of Twain,
Whitman, and Dreiser as strengths of an American as distinct from a
more subtle European tradition. The justification lies not just in the
world behind their art, for crudity surely has long existed in Europe,
but in the voice and forms they established as distinctly American
writers. Anderson valued the "barbaric yawp" of Whitman, disdained
the world of the literati, valued the role of the bard but felt the term
"poet" should never have been invented for a separate category of
human beings.[3]

Other essays take on social themes. "Notes on Standardization"
particularly laments American newspapers and magazines becoming
more alike and losing their individual voices—how much less then
than today, one might add. "I'll Say We've Done Well," a piece on
Ohio for *The Nation* (1922), wrestles with the energy and financial

success that have come to Ohio while the state has been turned from an attractive rural world into a center for ugly cities: Cleveland is "smugly self-satisfied." "King Coal" (1923) is a more explicit critique of the futility and despair brought to mining towns by mining and factories. An air of nostalgia intrudes as Anderson calls up from an earlier day an elderly carpetbagger, a delightful rascal who loved literature despite his sins. Now, however, all is standardized, ugly, and quietly desperate.

Surrounding these and a few other pieces are the autobiographical "Notes out of a Man's Life" and the opening "From Chicago," which while being the earliest drafted of all the sketches also serves to redefine the writer's life as beginning not in Clyde but in the big city. Recurring themes in the six sketches are writing, memory, and "the Negro," the passages on "the Negro" and New Orleans being tied to Anderson's preoccupation with the African American as healthy primitive, so prevalent in the writing of 1924 and 1925. The young man who opens "From Chicago" is a bit like George Willard seeking the possibilities of life and determining to make a book. In most of the other sketches there is a concern with the ubiquity of tale-telling, the difference between popular and serious fiction, the need for a writer to have patience, and the relationship among fancy, reality, memory, and fiction. Although Anderson was never a profound thinker, he often dwelt on the relationship among the several aspects of a writer's art. Perhaps the strongest piece in the book, in fact, is "A Meeting South," discussed above as the story about William Faulkner. It blends reality, memory, and fancy in an engaging New Orleans tale of David, the slim, heavily drinking man with a limp, and Aunt Sally, the elderly brothel keeper from the Midwest. It incorporates tales within tales, leaves the reader with a credible although fictionalized picture of Faulkner drunk and spreading false stories of his war experiences, but is also one of Anderson's most engaging fictions in his truest style.

HELLO TOWNS!

In his next two collections Anderson tried out two perspectives on America life. In *Hello Towns!* he is the Appalachian Virginia newspaper publisher, seeking among the farmers and mountaineers and through a fictional columnist "Buck Fever" a healthy viable outlook on his world and his career. In *Perhaps Women* he more prophetically hypothesizes that women provide the best hope for the country.

Hello Towns!, like *Sherwood Anderson's Notebook*, is a potpourri of earlier and new materials with recurring thematic motifs.[4] It is arranged by months, from November through October, like Thoreau's *Walden* organizing, in a year in the life of the author, reflections on a wide range of issues. The book's delight is in its random tales, sketches, and portraits rather than in its thematic continuity. Writing itself again is a central concern. Anderson introduces the book with another critique of Sinclair Lewis, a reminder that fiction is not a mere reflection of life, and with other justifications of the artist, and he begins "November" with praise of Dreiser and Twain as role models. Elsewhere he indicates his preference for George Borrow over Dickens and Thackeray, argues for a more "natural" mode of storytelling than one finds in the work of James Joyce, explores what the "education" of the artist can mean, but rejects any single set of rules for the writer and disdains college creative-writing programs. He concludes by grappling with issues of the "writer's trade" and the need to balance the demands of art with the demands of the market. He argues that there must even be an antidemocratic element to art, that in one sense the writer must be an aristocrat, an elitist, not socially or politically but artistically.

The emphasis on writing and art is balanced by an equal emphasis on the "reality" represented by the people of rural Virginia; the voice of Buck Fever with his vernacular perspective on those people, their politics and society; the inclusion of assorted blurbs on the school board, an elderly printer, a boxing match, the town pump (reminiscent of Hawthorne's sketch), and a little red-haired girl; and incorporation of the story of Joe, the mountaineer in "A Sentimental Journey," a fiction playing a different role here than it does in *Death in the Woods*, and of other engagingly developed tales of the region. One theme becomes the tension between the raw, crude, but at times gentle life of this rural world and the writer's attempt to transform it into literature whose significance is not simply the raw material itself.

The Buck Fever pieces included in *Hello, Towns!* are only part of Anderson's output under that name. Welford Dunaway Taylor has edited a splendid collection of all the Buck Fever pieces, as Ray

Lewis White earlier edited a wide range of pieces Anderson wrote for his two papers, the *Marion Democrat* and the *Smyth County News*.[5] Buck Fever, as Taylor shows, fits into the tradition of southwest humor and indeed of American humor going back to the Jack Downing letters out of Portland, Maine. He also is doubtless modeled on two of Anderson's Virginia friends, Andy Funk and Felix Sullivan. The colloquial humor of the Buck Fever papers adds a dimension to Anderson's accomplishment as a cultural and social critic of the United States between the two world wars.[6] It provided him with a new voice, a voice with a southern slant, as the innocent outsider looking at small-town life. Some of the scenes are vividly and poignantly captured, but the more general reflections on social issues are shallow and impercipient. The book, of course, includes the predictable Anderson polemics against standardization, the age of the machine, modern cities, and "mass man." The most embarrassing passage today is an early one, in "December," in which the author denies any interest in racial integration or equality but seeks "merely justice" for the American Negro. Anderson particularly decries northern "reformers" who come down to interfere. In cities, he says, the Negro "doesn't sing any more" (63) as he did on the land. In another passage in "December" he writes, "there has been in me always something calling from the north, a voice calling from the south. In regard to the negro I am Southern. I have no illusions about making him my brother" (54–55). Lest the picture of his racial attitudes be too unbalanced, however, it should be added that Anderson wrote an engaging story, never published but in the Newberry Library collection, about an attempted lynching that is quite critical of American racism, and he also wrote an introductory essay to the catalogue for an art show of paintings related to lynchings.[7] Lynchings, of course, like slavery a century earlier, were an easy target for northerners not otherwise critical of racism.

PERHAPS WOMEN

Hello Towns! marks just about the last significant incidence of Anderson's special interest in the African American as the symbol of vitality in an increasingly standardized America. He continues his interest in the mountaineer and farmer as sources of such symbolism, but for a period he explores the female principle as a saving hope. There had always been in Anderson a tension between a conventional male view of female inferiority in many walks of life including art and a baffled fascination with the strength of women he knew, including, of course, Gertrude Stein and Babs Finley. He failed to bring coherence to his one early female portrait, Mary Cochran, but in several of his novels strong women do influence the direction of the story. Then, certainly, Eleanor Copenhaver changed not only his politics but also his views of gender. Surely he recalled, moreover, Henry Adams's articulation of the female principle as a lost unifying force, as in "The Virgin and the Dynamo." In any case, *Perhaps Women* posits that American men have been defeated by the age of the machine and are now, in fact, impotent and no longer good for women, and that the only hope for America lies in the vitality of its women. In his Introduction Anderson asserts a "growing conviction that modern man is losing his ability to retain his manhood in the face of the modern way of utilizing the machine and that what hope there is for him lies in women."[8] He calls his new form an "impression" or a "sketch" rather than a collection of essays. It mixes a highly and rather self-consciously lyrical prose with more straightforward essaylike sections.

Perhaps Women, however, reads more like an elegy for the lost, defeated, castrated male than a brief for feminism. In a similar way, of course, Anderson's earlier paeans to the "American Negro" are more an elegy for a white race dehumanized and sapped by the machine age than a plea for racial justice; and romanticizing the Virginia mountaineer is more an acknowledgment of decadence and sterility in cities and factory towns than a serious argument for his backwoods heroes to be taken as role models for a new generation.

Perhaps Women revolves almost entirely around southern mill workers, although the prose at times echoes the romantic cadences of *Mid-American Chants* and its midwestern cornfields. The southern factories are, on the one hand, additional examples of dehumanizing industrialization, but, on the other hand, the home base of the women who at least symbolically give Anderson hope. As a consequence there is more ambivalence toward factories and machines in *Perhaps Women* than in his other books. There is a place for citing Whitman, Sandburg, and their hymns to industry. There is a set of detailed and hardly pejorative descriptions of looms at work, of the wonder of machines, of the complexity of the mill. If "bitch success" drives the system, if the boring sameness of houses defines a mill town, if the mill is really a vast prison—all motifs in *Perhaps Women,* still the not unsympathetic mill owner and the young mill superintendent are engaging figures of the New South, and the women who work in the mills are strong, capable, and full of a new kind of potential energy. Anderson does not resolve the inconsistency in the book: there is no real connection made between on the one hand the machine world of the cotton mills—or automobile factories, for that matter—that symbolize the crushing defeat of the male and on the other hand a romance of the American woman as her country's last best hope. The book keeps asking, "Is it a woman's age?" and saying "Perhaps women," but never does Anderson convey what this would mean. The mill girl in Georgia does not lead to any more significant image of a positive force than do the African Americans along the Mississippi River in *Dark Laughter.*

PUZZLED AMERICA

Four years later Anderson came out with *Puzzled America.* As *Perhaps Women* was written at the beginning of the Great Depression, *Puzzled America* was written in its depths. Anderson had no new answers. The book openly expresses a hunger for belief, for faith in something. It teems with portraits of unemployed workers—miners, electricians, farmers, machinists—and with pictures of poverty, of wandering lost souls, of women and men and children. Very much a period piece from the Depression, at times a poignant period piece, it includes twelve sketches from the South, four from the Midwest, and a concluding section, "What the Woman Said," that puts American despair into a larger world context. Along with *Beyond Desire* this is Anderson's Depression text, and in the end *Puzzled America* is more optimistic than the novel. If Anderson is surprised, throughout his travels, to keep finding that peculiar American optimism surfacing in the face of defeat, he himself replicates it in the book if only by contrast with a Europe that has "no smiles" left at all.

The midwestern sketches are brighter than those set in the South. Anderson opens in southern coal-mining country, where miners can be both pathetic and magnificent, where communism has had its attractions for exploited workers but where nonetheless antidemocratic ideologies still cannot take hold. The book moves from the mines to mill towns and then farm land, farm land exploited and abused by the scions of an old aristocracy and mill towns where machines clearly outweigh concern about human life. A section called "People" includes vivid portraits of down-and-outers and of the "tall straight men" of Tennessee Valley Authority (TVA) country.[9] Two sketches touch on the hope provided by the New Deal, outline a possible new "social view" in America, and also suggest that the Depression may push America beyond its destructive selfishness. Other sketches reflect the antiunion sentiment of southern mill towns and the "new tyrant class" of the South, the children of poverty who, like Faulkner's Flem Snopes one might have said a few years later, survive to buy up land and business and who brutally exploit labor with no more sense of responsibility than the powerful men who once oppressed their fathers. A poignant sketch of "Elizabethton, Tennessee" depicts a town whose buildings are but five years old yet already decrepit and filthy, whose young women in the rayon plants are heroic but get old rapidly.[10]

Toward the end of the southern section are portraits of "The Nationalist," an American out for big profits and hating regulatory laws and reformers; of less fortunate people, who blame themselves for their failures; and then at the end of Rush Holt, a candidate from West Virginia for the United States Senate, an able and smart legislator who if nothing else brings the section to a conclusion that is more optimistic, if tentative, than most of the book has been. Grandson of a Union sympathizer, son of a fighter for radical causes, Holt comes from hill people and retains their strength but along with abilities and intelligence and education and virtues suited to the modern world.

The positive figure who concludes the book's middle or Midwest section is very different, Floyd Olson, a governor elected against the wishes of the power elite in Minnesota. Anderson's Midwest, the locus of much of his fiction, never seems quite as bleak as his South of coal mines and mill towns. "Revolt in South Dakota" suggests the state may be willing to grow out of its traditional conservatism, and "Olsonville" suggests the region is more prepared than others to throw overboard narrow party allegiances and political structures and paranoia about "socialism." Back in the Midwest, Anderson once again uses "corn" as a symbol of nostalgia and vitality. These sketches are also full of colorful vignettes—of tenant farmers, printers, taverns, people who have lost homes, church meetings—as well as stories within stories. *Puzzled America* is still puzzled, but in 1935 Anderson can articulate the patient optimism depended on by New Deal orators even when his short individual sketches at times seem closer to the pessimistic or even apocalyptic despair of so much serious American fiction of the day.

The book ends with "The Return of the Princess," a plea by a Polish ex-princess for the United States not to throw away its democratic traditions for a dictatorship, not to yield to the despair she finds in Europe, but rather to build on hope and the meaning "America" has for the peoples of the world. It could as easily be Anderson himself speaking, after his search through the two regions where he has found, throughout his career, both the bleakness of modern anomie and the vitality of American hope. *Puzzled America* comes halfway between Anderson's last two novels, *Beyond Desire* and *Kit Brandon*, one being Anderson's last attempt at a quasi-tragic perspective on conflict in America and the other being a positive portrayal of a hill country woman from the perspective of a puzzled and awestruck authorial narrator. Married to Eleanor, engaged in hopeful endeavors, mellowing, Anderson during the dark years of the Depression sought redemption in American vitality and optimism even if he never lost the ability to capture poignantly images of the country's voiceless and homeless and hopeless people.

No Swank

Anderson's other book during this period was *No Swank*, a collection of seventeen sketches or "impressions" as he calls them, of persons, mostly but not only Americans, from his own life, varied but all in one way or another leaving behind a positive image or positive influence. The subjects include writers like Theodore Dreiser, or "*the* Dreiser" as Anderson calls his role model; Gertrude Stein, "great because she is a releaser of talent. She is a path-finder" (84), and she has "taught all of us" (82);[11] D. H. Lawrence, who so well represented a "very clean maleness" of the artist; George Borrow; Ring Lardner; and Paul Rosenfeld, "the man among our critics most sensitive and creatively alive." Also here are Margaret Anderson, associated with the Chicago renaissance; Lincoln Steffens, associated with political idealism; and an unnamed New York painter and J. J. Hawkes, a talented Virginia woodcut artist. Jack Dempsey rather than the "patronizing" Gene Tunney represents the athlete as artist, although one might note that in 1937 Anderson also wrote a very positive essay on Joe Louis.[12] Four sketches reflect personal ties with the less famous and artistic—Leon Bazalgette, who appreciated Anderson's work and visited him in his illness; George W. Sells, who fought beside Stonewall Jackson at Chancellorsville; Jasper Deeter, a friend from the world of theater; and two Irishmen full of tenderness and vitality. The titular essay is of Henry Wallace, like Rush Holt and Floyd Olson a political hope for moving America ahead. Beneath the book is also a view of life that what is most lasting in one's sense of self and identity are the cumulative *impressions* from one's life as they stick in the memory. To some extent *No Swank* is a nonfictive counterpart in Anderson's life to *Winesburg, Ohio*, the sequence of "impressions" that shape his most famous fictional town.

HOME TOWN

One irony of Anderson's career is that his final published work, *Home Town* (1940), included in *The Sherwood Anderson Reader* (1947) in its longer form as "The American Small Town," is a repudiation not so much of *Winesburg, Ohio* as of the common reading of *Winesburg* as anti–small town, as a cardinal text of the "revolt against the village." While the corrective interpretations of David Anderson and others have made a difference, nonetheless it is natural to read that book and other early Anderson fiction with a sense of his probable disdain for the provinciality of small towns, even as he early on displayed distaste for urban sterility as well. *Home Town*, however, is a hymn to the American village, doubtless building on his affection for Marion, Virginia, but testifying that New England and Midwest towns are the "backbone" of America, the fount of democracy, the source of American hope and optimism—even in American cities, made up in part of former villagers.

Much of the essay is built again on the seasons—spring, summer, fall, winter—as they provide the settings for sentimental but colorful impressions and sketches of village life. There is the predictable criticism of factories changing small town life, but the strength of the work lies in its impressions—fire trucks going to fires, front-porch sitting, circuses, town eccentrics and "types," the tobacco market, high school football games, small town jury trials and the dramas of everyday life, skating on the pond, and so forth. It is a remarkable eulogy and memoir, perhaps analogous to *Winesburg* as *The Reivers* is to *The Sound and the Fury* in Faulkner's career. It has that elegiac winsomeness, detected also in *Kit Brandon,* of a world honored but disappearing. By the end of Anderson's career the "positive" endings have evolved from an image of a young man fleeing constraints to seek a hopeful if uncertain future, to a middle-aged person fleeing constraints out of self-indulgence, to a wider community sense of the good. Anderson never rejected the value of the individual life and identity, but like Emerson as he aged he came to see a larger value and meaning for the self in the broader community.[13]

7

Autobiographies

IN ANDERSON'S STUDY AT THE TIME OF HIS DEATH WERE A SET OF pieces on the craft of writing that he was calling "The Writer's Book" and an unfinished set of memoirs. The memoirs were posthumously published in 1942 as edited by Paul Rosenfeld, who also included much of "The Writer's Book," and then in 1969 issued in a more complete, and critical, edition prepared by Ray Lewis White.[1] It is instructive to read the memoirs in relation to *A Story-Teller's Story*, Anderson's first autobiography, but also in relation to the more deliberately fictional *Tar* and the personal sections of *Sherwood Anderson's Notebook*, discussed above.

A Story-Teller's Story is an engaging and intriguing work. Like *Winesburg, Ohio* it does not depend on a coherent conceptual structure so much as on building a cumulative effect from discrete but related parts. It is a created self, not a memoir, like Jean-Paul Sartre's *The Words* a work designed to be emotionally and psychologically valid, not a chronicle designed to be factually accurate and complete. John Crowley interprets it as a rebuttal of *The Education of Henry Adams*, tracing a progress not a series of failures.[2] The influence of Adams is clearly there, although Anderson's work lacks the rich historical texture found in *The Education*. It is a "tale of an American writer's journey through his own imaginative world and through the world of facts," in effect a created self and a created cultural portrayal by a writer in middle age and mid-career putting himself into an artistic tradition and justifying himself through a developmental paradigm.[3] Although Henry Adams is an influential precursor whom Anderson frequently mentions, *A Story-Teller's Story* fits into a tradition of created American selves from Ben Franklin through Frederick Douglass, Mark Twain, and Adams and looking ahead to Gertrude Stein (*Autobiography of Alice B. Toklas*), Richard Wright, and others whose constructed life stories take on peculiarly "American" characteristics.

The book provides little factual biographical data such as that found in, for example, Kim Townsend's biography or Anderson's later memoirs. It tells the spiritual journey of an American craftsman and artist and, like *Winesburg*, it engages the reader mostly because of the characters one meets and the impressions of their lives and feelings. At times the narrator is, like George Willard, a listener and observer, but at other times he spins out self-consciously at age fifty what he sees as the central factors in his emotional and intellectual growth. At the very beginning Anderson insists that these "notes make no pretense of being a record of fact" but aim "to be true to the essence of things"; otherwise we will "let our fancies loose" (100). Later he comments on the genre of "autobiography, even of the half-playful sort I am now attempting" (257).

A Story-Teller's Story is divided into four "books," each consisting of seven to fifteen "notes" or sections. Each book revolves around, successively, youth and parentage, young manhood and the discovery of self, vocation and the American artist, and commitment to craft in a larger context.[4] The central figure in Book I is Anderson's father, here a collage of invention, myth, fact, and fancy. The father, in fact, is so central that the boy seems at times forgotten, and it may be for that reason that Anderson wrote *Tar*, a fictive account of his own childhood, one in which the boy's story remains central. Anderson in his fiction had already worked through the internal conflicts he felt over his father, but in *A Story-Teller's Story* these are replayed as the central dynamic of his fantasies. Father is the "ruined dandy," the storyteller, the showman, the singer and dancer, the liar, a man the son hates and the mother would like to hang. From this book a reader could hardly learn that Irwin Anderson was a harness maker and house painter. The reader would learn, however, that the author liked to imagine a "father of fancy," a Civil War spy, an arms smuggler in South American revolutions, as an alternative to the real father. One also could learn that, despite the father's flaws and the son's resentment, I "would be loath to trade him for a more provident, shrewd and thoughtful father" (47). Sherwood Anderson, as a professional teller of tales, knows that he is truly his father's son: "There were tales to be told and he was the teller of tales" (55). He gladly subscribes to the refrain of his father's song, "You grow more like your dad every day" (75). Mother, for all of Anderson's love for her and for her being the one who really raised the family, is in this book a cameo portrait—tall, slender, *once* beautiful, and then dead at an early age. She is more important for her own mother, a dark evil old woman who although in reality German here is the source of the imagined Italian blood that provides Anderson with a romantic past.

Father, however, is in the story mostly for some Civil War adventures, more fancy than fact. His is the story of a southern boy loyal to the Union, the trapped prisoner of war helped by a sister and a slave to escape both rebel officers and the tough mother who would gladly hang her son for treason, the soldier at Gettysburg learning of the death of his family. This is the main character in Book I. The book may be about the contrast between fancy and fact, but it is also about creating one's past in the act of establishing one's identity. To some extent Anderson traces his interest in writing to his attempt to replace his father, the raconteur who never learned that tales could be written as well as recited. So he both imitates his father and replaces him. As in childhood he and his brothers replayed the Leatherstocking Tales, the romantic battles of Natty Bumppo, Uncas, and *Le Renard Subtil*, so in maturity Anderson will live his romance vicariously through his writing.[5]

In Book II Anderson is the teenager and young adult, not yet the writer, although an avid reader, but developing his identity. That development takes place in large part through relationships with three persons—Nora, daughter of his landlord; "Judge" Turner; and Alonzo Berners. Each episode is presented as factual not invented, but each is also described as a "literary" triumph or failure. The book describes Anderson's work in a warehouse and in the stables of a viciously anti-Catholic man, Nate Lovett. Its main interest, however, lies in Anderson's curious relationship with Nora the housekeeper, over whom he establishes dominance, worth clean sheets every day to him, until he lies to her about his fight with a star athlete. She is smart enough to know that Anderson is lying, that he cannot admit his defeat in a fight, and in the end she is stronger than he. The "failed literary story" teaches Anderson the boundaries between lying and storytelling. Meanwhile the fascinating Arthur Turner, called "Judge," enchants young Sherwood with tales "no doubt as true as these confessions of myself . . . I am setting down here. What I mean is that he was at least trying to inject into them the essence of truth" (162). They may, of course, be as "true" as Father's tales of the Civil War. Son of a suicidal Presbyterian minister in a small Ohio town, Turner had fantasized his father as a fifteenth-century cardinal or pope or a wicked Italian Medici, and himself as a Duke Francisco. Fascinated by stories of their cruelty and use of poison, he picked, dried, and carried in his own pocket a vial of lethal herbs, giving himself the feeling of a newfound power. Like Anderson he made a mistake with a star athlete, sending him an ill-planned note with flowers, and thereby ruined his own college years. Turner, too, learned to sublimate his impulses and accept a less romantic life but one with the stability provided by money and respect.

In some ways Twain's *Roughing It* is the book most like *A Story-Teller's Story*, a tale of the future writer trying on other hats and other faces and then realizing that he is to be a writer, "an almighty scribbler." As in Twain's book, periodic social comments dot the autobiography, in this case snide attacks on standardization, factories, Henry Ford, and the loss of individualism. Anderson, like Twain, and not unlike Henry Adams, laments that he was not born into the fifteenth century, the age of the Borgias: "How I longed to be a richly gowned, soft-handed cunning but scholarly grandee and patron of the arts" (252).

Alonzo Berners, son of Chicago merchant Jim Berners, is an invalid who drinks too much and leaves himself vulnerable and helpless before "cheap thugs" on the street and in the bars. Anderson, ironically, learns from his own assistance to Berners a kind of love, a growing up "to the realization that oneself did not matter" in the larger picture. For Anderson it is learning the importance of the other, "the rediscovery of man by man," in a world where one had "no God, the gods having been taken from me by the life about me" (270). Alonzo dies soon afterward but not without having played a role in this story. The final sections of Book II, on Anderson's months in the Spanish-American War, may seem irrelevant here, but they are an attempt on the heels of Alonzo's story to show the narrator committing himself to something larger than himself.

Books III and IV together make up the final third of *A Story-Teller's Story*. Book III, much the shorter of the two, narrates Anderson's emerging career-commitment and self-consciousness of that commitment: "I had become a writer, a word-fellow. That was my craft" (327). Anderson sets advertising and his first career, a form of "prostitution" (307), explicitly against his art and craft. He sets the honest teller of tales against the purveyor of "glad sentimental romances" (308). He sets the American writer striving to become an artist against the European, who works in a culture where the arts play an established role. In America, obsessed with its own special destiny, people do not want to hear of those human themes that connect us with the rest of mankind, for we fear "to find ourselves at the end no more brave, heroic and fine than the people of almost any other part of the world" (31). The book also sets scenes from Anderson's youth, and a return to some of them, against what he sees not only as a new maturity but also as a new self now linked to storytelling going back to Old Norse and the Hebrew Bible.

Book IV carries Anderson from the Midwest to New York. It is more an artistic manifesto than part of an autobiography. There are scenes set in restaurants and rooming houses, but Book IV is the author's self-definition and self-justification. He is the self-conscious midwesterner, different from but relating to Easterners and Europeans. Although unlike the *Seven Arts* crowd, he can still be part of a larger rebellion of modernism against "plot" and other old conventions of form. He can assert the bond to visual artists felt by his contemporaries but reject the special romantic setting-off of artists by their society. Perhaps the most memorable visual image in the book is hands, the hands that for him symbolize the craft that is the sine qua non for any artist: "The arts are after all but the old crafts intensified, followed with religious fervor and determination by men who love them" (327). Passages in Notes V and VI recall the story of Wing Biddlebaum, "Hands," and add a poignantly ironic note to a reader's reflection on it.

Anderson is proud to be part of a new movement in the arts; but as a midwesterner he also feels as awkwardly rough as Henry Adams felt outdated as a New Englander. He also feels the attraction of his contemporaries to Paris, where one can be quite comfortable just sitting and writing, as one may not feel in the bustling, business-of-America-is-business United States. Whether in Chartres or New York, however, whether recalling an episode from his boyhood or sitting in his room with fellow writer "Arthur Hobson," he moves toward a quiet conclusion, romantic yet ironic. The final image is that of his Balzac volume, unintentionally damaged by his friend during a nervous dialogue: "From the floor of my room the name Balzac is grinning ironically up into my own American face" (442).

TAR: A MIDWEST CHILDHOOD

Tar should be counted as one of Anderson's eight novels, or nine if *Winesburg, Ohio* is also read as a novel. It is always considered a fictional account of the author's youth, but despite our cataloguing *A Story-Teller's Story* as autobiography, it has about the same connection to biography that *Tar* does. Certainly *Tar*, as Anderson admits, allows him to re-create his childhood conflicts and crises in a fictive fantasy, but it is misleading to read Tar literally as young Sherwood. Even the father, Dick Moorehead, is an additional fictive version of Irwin Anderson, an unwitting abolitionist but to be sure a harness shop owner and house painter as well. The psychological conflicts of baby siblings entering the house, of town bullies, of a first awareness of death ("Death in the Woods" appearing here in one of its several forms), of awakening sexuality, of near-poverty and friends who are better off, of the end of childhood—all play a part in *Tar*.

In a foreword to *Tar* Anderson indicates that we can never trust a writer with truth, for "Truth is impossible to me," since like any writer he will make fictions out of facts and constantly recreate life in the field of fancy.[6] "The teller of tales . . . lives in a world of his own," and "All tale telling is, in a strict sense, nothing but lying. . . . To tell the truth is too difficult. I long since gave up the effort" (7–8). And so the fictional characters are never real people, but here I have created "a Tar Moorehead to stand for myself. . . . It is, I admit, a writer's trick" (10). Thus Edgar "Tar" Moorehead, child of a North Carolina father become Ohio abolitionist simply because in Ohio that is politically correct.

The tension between fancy and fact remains central to the story of young Tar: "All the best things for a boy are always imagined" (63). Resentment over new siblings is more important than resentment of the father. There are illnesses and deaths, fears and fantasies, experiences being reshaped in the fancy. There is a growing awareness of sex and difficulty dealing with it. Tar has an alternate family, Hal Brown's, and he feels warmer and more comfortable with them than at home. Things get confusing in the boy's mind as a "bad" prostitute does good things, a smelly and dishonest hog-buyer turns out to be a most sensitive person, and a boxer who might be a hero turns out to be a villain. At the end, still living between fact and fancy, still unsure what it all means, mourning the death of Mary Moorehead, Tar cries himself out in no small part because at least the author if not Tar himself knows he has also come to the end of his childhood.

MEMOIRS

When Anderson in the 1930s began to put together notes for his memoirs, his intent was very different from the one he had when writing *A Story-Teller's Story*. Where there is very little factual external information in the earlier book, the memoirs are full of actual remembered incidents and personal data. They are not, to be sure, the same as a biography. There is still very little on Anderson's wives and children and only selected episodes about his siblings. The memoirs do, however, incorporate many impressions of and reflections on people and experiences from his actual past. They provide more or less a record of moments, not a continuum; but in that light it is useful to recall a comment from *A Story-Teller's Story* that "as a tale-teller I have come to think that the true history of life is but a history of moments. It is only at rare moments that we live" (309). In *Winesburg, Ohio* and his other best fiction, the impressions of moments most effectively engage readers, and so it is in his nonfiction as well.

In a preface to his memoirs Anderson says that he is "not so much wanting to make the picture of the life of a man as of a certain period in American life" (3).[7] He says in his foreword that he will use his own life "as a springboard" and that this will be a "book of the mind and imagination," a tale told as if to a friend walking "on a country road" (29). It has a rambling quality, but if it is a work of the "imagination," it is still tied far more to the facts of Anderson's experience than is the more fabricated growth of an emotional self in *A Story-Teller's Story*. It is also important to remember that Anderson was never able to prepare the book for publication. Rather it has only appeared as edited first by Paul Rosenfeld, assisted by Roger Sergel and Eleanor Anderson, and later by Ray White. As White, working through more than three thousand pages of manuscript, realized, Rosenfeld did rewrite passages in order to produce a more coherent whole.[8] Even if Anderson himself had not described the memoirs as a set of impressions rather than as a unified whole, any comment on structure has to acknowledge the work's unfinished state. There is about the first parts—on childhood, young adulthood, the years in business and in Chicago—more sense of form than in the final sections on Anderson's last two decades, which jump more awkwardly from, for example, a short essay on publishers or on Carl Sandburg to another on the Bonus Army or people of color. The last parts are in a decidedly unfinished state, yet not without interest, while the first half of the memoirs includes some of Anderson's best writing.

As published the *Memoirs* have six chapters—"Childhood and Young Manhood," "Work and War," "Business," "Chicago," "The Twenties," and "The Thirties." The first chapter is notably gentle on Anderson's father while expressing resentment at the family's poverty and remembered shame at the need of his mother to take in laundry. It includes touching vignettes of youthful friends such as Jimmy Moore and Herman Hurd, of Sneaky Pete the ne'er-do-well who each morning shouted to the town the names of local philanderers, and of Sherwood's relationship to his sister, Stella. It provides insight into his time in the livery stable and bicycle factory and confesses his deep desire then to become rich but, perhaps less persuasively, suggests that even then he was distressed by the equating of influence with money and the loss of earlier values of craft and workmanship.

The second chapter does provide details on Anderson's war experience, not a positive picture of the army, and thumbnail sketches of several fascinating figures, but the recurring theme is Anderson's sense of his own slickness in the business world and his increasing feeling that he was often dirty and dishonest in being slick. The third chapter, "Business," continues this theme, of slickness as sickness, and of writing being the route to honesty. On the other hand, the emerging righteousness is of a piece with self-indulgent introspection that allows him to dismiss wife and children, as John Webster in

Many Marriages can dehumanize his wife and as Irwin Anderson at Emma's death could desert his family. The writer in his enlightenment can say, "No man, in his heart, can really believe in rugged individualism, this superman stuff for most business is done under the table" (245), but then can, in saying that he, "I, Sherwood Anderson, was going to be different," deny the reality of the self that had evolved over several decades. By tying his wife to the business world and middle-class conventions and his own resentments he can pretend to have started over, to be an Adamic self, a writer, an artist, naked in the new world, no longer prostituting himself to deceive people, even if possibly deceiving himself.

The fourth chapter, "Chicago," carries that commitment into Anderson's actual work as a writer, one of "We little children of the arts" in Chicago's "Robin's Egg Renaissance." It is a nostalgic portrayal of a happy time shared by struggling artists, comradely in the face of an America some saw as tearing its citizens apart. The chapter captures some poignant images, for example, of the large painter named Ben, a tall prostitute, a Russian Jewish immigrant who since coming to the States had experienced success and devastating failure, the Italian poet Emmanuel Carnevali, Anderson's friends at the Dill Pickle Club, and the tragic drowning of Ann Mitchell in Lake Michigan shortly after her marriage to Anderson's friend Jack Jones. The author meanwhile articulates the emergence of his own aesthetic values as he recalled it. Extolling Twain and Melville as America's greatest writers, he says that he realized writing had gotten too far away from a felt and lived life and required a new boldness of speech that could be a kind of painting in prose (338). Lamenting again both what he called the Puritan influence on American writing and the "so much whoredom" deriving from commercial influences on language and literature, he emphasizes the importance of *Winesburg, Ohio* to his life—the epiphany he had in the process of writing "Hands," and the role of his Chicago experience in the creation of the characterizations in the book.[9]

The final two chapters have splendid sections although without as many functional connections between the parts. There are more fine sketches—of Old Mary, the overweight and aging former actress who is Anderson's landlady around 1921; of Theodore Dreiser, a "great and honest writer" despite personal and literary flaws; of Horace Liveright; of Faulkner and Hemingway and Fitzgerald and Paul

Green and other writers. There are tidbits and anecdotes and random comments on Anderson's own writing and episodes from travel. Ray Lewis White has done all Anderson readers a lasting service in making the *Memoirs* available in a form readable but as close to what Anderson left us as possible, for scattered throughout truly are some of his best and most moving passages of prose.

8

The Final Novels

SHERWOOD ANDERSON'S LAST TWO NOVELS REPRESENT TWO ATTEMPTS to take a different direction in fiction. In *Kit Brandon* he used the technique Scott Fitzgerald had used in *The Great Gatsby* and that other novelists have used effectively, first-person narration by a secondary character of a story about a more mysterious titular character with the narrator himself gradually becoming as interesting and as important a figure as the main character. *Beyond Desire* was Anderson's one attempt at a political novel, and it really does not turn out to be a very political novel at all.

BEYOND DESIRE

The basic format of *Beyond Desire* is similar to that of other Anderson novels, notably *Poor White* and *Dark Laughter*. In all three cases the story of the primary male character is interrupted by, or counterpointed against, the story of a primary female character whose life intertwines with his. In *Poor White* the stories of Hugh McVey and Clara Butterworth culminate in a strange marriage. In *Dark Laughter* the stories of Bruce Dudley and Aline Grey end in an equally bizarre affair. In *Beyond Desire* the one act of sexual intimacy, between Red Oliver and Ethel Long, is the only scene of affection in the book and terminates rather than develops their relationship. Their stories maintain a loose thematic connection.

Following his early manuscripts of young persons seeking their way in life, and then two novels of midlife crises, Anderson in 1932 published his first novel influenced by his relationship with Eleanor

110

and by a new political sensitivity. To be sure, his nonfiction of the period reflects a deeper concern with workers, the alienation at the heart of industrialization and standardization, and the potential of women to redeem America. Scenes in *Beyond Desire* suggest a more deeply felt response to the plight of workers; but although the book is included among those inspired—like Grace Lumphin's *To Make My Bread* (1932) and Mary Heaton Vorse's *Strike* (1930)—by the tragic Gastonia textile strike of 1929, the only moving labor scenes are set in a Georgia town where most of the story is set, not in the North Carolina town where it ends with Red's death.

Beyond Desire, moreover, is neither a proletarian nor an ideological novel. Neither Red Oliver nor the author ever commits himself to communism or to the labor cause. Their sympathies are with workers, not mill owners, and a voice within Red near the end suggests communism may be the answer. He is not convinced, however, and his act of stepping forth to his death results from impulse, not conviction. Nor does Anderson deal seriously with a political argument for communism or labor, as one finds in, for example, Richard Wright's *Native Son* and John Steinbeck's *In Dubious Battle*. The subject down to the end, in fact, remains the difficulty that a bright and well-meaning youth has making a meaningful commitment to a career or to a cause. The cynicism that accompanies Ethel Long's rejection of Red and impulsive marriage to Tom Parker is of a piece with the bafflement of Red finding his way to the communist cause. The title that might well fit his story is the one Thomas Wolfe wished to use for his first book, "O Lost!"

Instead the title is *Beyond Desire*, and both Ethel and Red take actions at the end of their stories—there is a further epilogue to Ethel's—that grow out of a frustration that follows desire. Whereas Red is the central character in the beginning and the end of the novel, Ethel's story is contained by and large in the third section. The female counterpoint to Red's story in the first half of the novel is a role played by Doris Hoffman and her mill-worker friends. At the end the role is played by Molly Seabright, the Carolina farm girl become mill worker, fascinated by one Red Oliver who calls himself a "communist." Both she and Red are starved for love, but fate does not allow them more than a brief acquaintance.

Beyond Desire is divided into four books—"Youth," "Mill Girls," "Ethel," and "Beyond Desire," the first and fourth carrying Red's story. Red grows up in Langdon, Georgia, a cotton mill town. Red's grandfather was a successful and respected physician, his father, like many Anderson fathers, a failure, albeit as a physician. His mother, a nurse from a lower-class Atlanta family, is scorned by townspeople and turns for support to an evangelical Methodist church frequented by poor whites. This section of Georgia is both a part of a tired Old South, one basis for Ethel Long's cynicism, and a part of the New South of Henry Grady, a boom town with a successful cotton mill, run by Tom Shaw. Shaw is a stalwart Presbyterian, not a sweaty Methodist, although he is not above enlisting a charismatic Methodist preacher-orator as collaborator to convert the citizens of Langdon to support for the new economy. The mill was built on false promises, child labor, and crowded, unhealthy conditions, but it provides a living of sorts to its workers and a good living to its owner.

Red, a college boy with a talent for baseball, is hired at the mill for the summer, only because Shaw intervenes in order to help the son of a good family. Through the job Red becomes confused and déclassé. He is attracted to the female workers, admires the working-class superintendent, is fascinated by the machines, and is contemptuous of Shaw. The experience has a lyrical and a quasi-sexual quality tied both to the workers and their machines and to the "Negro." There are very few persons of color in the book, but Red recalls a time when as a child he was attracted to a bed with a matronly breasted black woman and her lover rather than to the bed of his own mother, who is mocked by the black people as well as the white (64–65).[1] One of Red's most important decisions at work is to play on the mill workers' baseball team, not the town team whose players come from his own social class. He is a star, but never feels he belongs and is, in effect, wed to his discontent.

Book Two, "Mill Girls," revolves around Doris Hoffman and the mill workers, particularly Nell, Fanny, and Grace. It is the strongest section of the book, drawing on Anderson's skill at impressionistic sketches rather than character development.[2] An "essay" on bobbins (84) and descriptions of the fall fair capture the atmosphere of a paternalistic mill. The fair, like baseball, provides a rare escape for mill workers, whose lives are "walled in" and who themselves are often, like Grace, tubercular or, like Ed Hoffman, physically weak. Doris is the heroic one, illiterate and frustrated but capable, strong, and good. Like the implicit women of *Perhaps Women* she is a positive alternative to the inept males in the book, but in the world of *Beyond Desire* she has no room to develop a life and will go down with the other workers who lose their jobs.

Book Three tells the story of Ethel Long, and at the beginning Anderson explicitly calls up the theme of *Perhaps Women*: men having failed in America, women are now needed to fill the breach (148). Ethel is the "modern woman," not the "lady," implying her rejection of if not the general demise of the southern myth of the spotless white lady. Although daughter of a conservative judge, Ethel repudiates the Old South, religion, and the conventions of Langdon. She graduates from the University of Chicago, and while part of a literary circle in Chicago—Sandburg, Masters, Maxwell Bodenheim are all mentioned—she finds little satisfaction there. She will find little satisfaction anywhere. Like Red she is a romantic lost in the modern world. A tall, straight, even mannish woman, "she had been in revolt ever since she came to Chicago" (152). Nurtured on novels of Balzac and George Moore, she nonetheless loses interest in everything but wealth and perhaps marriage to a rich man with "swank." She comes to have contempt for a philosophy instructor, Harold Grey, who is attracted to her. Then she is led to Fred Wells, a patent-medicine drummer, a midwestern Mephistopheles and sadist who tries to rape her. Fred is drawn impressionistically, through his thoughts, which reveal him to be a frustrated and coarse egotist full of contempt for everyone else and filled with "a bright shining hatred" (172). His brutality drives Ethel back to Georgia but does not cure her of a taste for scoundrels.

Tom Riddle is a smoother scoundrel, a scheming, "cigar-smoking," successful lawyer-politician with contempt for churchgoers and reformers. A widower, he seeks a woman to "decorate" his life and Ethel, he says, has "style" (194). He is a Republican because money rules, and in the North the Republicans are "the money crowd." At forty-five he is much older than Ethel, who herself is much older than Red. Ethel's ambivalence about Red and Tom is like Red's about commitment. Anderson uses his common, at times trite, device of, for example, "She was resentful. . . . She was not resentful" (214), to convey Ethel's uncertainty. One rainy night she gives herself sexually to Red (after reading Marx!), but then she is confused, he is ashamed, and nobody is happy. Ethel will finally leave home and marry her fellow "realist" Tom, or at least "try it." Only at the very end, when Red's body is buried back in Langdon will her still latent desire for something romantic again emerge.

Ethel has had one other conflict, with her father's young decadent second wife Blanche, who stays in bed smoking most days until noon. The bad blood between them, however, culminates in Blanche's aggressive lesbian caress of and assault on Ethel, during which Blanche confesses she has really loved Ethel all along. In horror Ethel, whose original description suggests some gender ambivalence, resists her and soon moves out of the house. Professor Grey, Fred Wells, Red Oliver, Blanche—why not try marriage with Tom Riddle, "beyond desire"?

Meanwhile by November of that year, 1930, Red finds himself in the strikers' camp in Birchfield, North Carolina, although it is never clear just why or how. There was a failed strike at the mill in Langdon, through which Red, although fleeing town, remained ambivalent ideologically. The mill workers falsely believed that he fought with the owners; he never admitted he was with the workers at the time of the struggle. In a cowardly way he finally slipped away. Red was also upset that Ethel has made a fool out of him, and he was more obsessed with her than with the mill owners. He is driven to his fatal end in North Carolina by four factors. First is the experience with Ethel that leaves him confused and in flight. Second is a despicable salesman near Birchfield who gives him a ride and goads him into saying he is one with the strikers. Third is the attractive woman with the cow on the hill, Molly Seabright, who wants to believe Red a communist come to make things better. Finally, there are the associations he draws between the strikers' camp and Methodist camp meetings of his childhood, which inspired believers to fervor and action. Red also has in his background a friendship with a college roommate, Neil Bradley, a dedicated Marxist; but he is aware that when the communists get involved in a labor action they are often unscrupulous exploiters and will even get workers killed in order to develop sympathy for their cause.

Molly Seabright and Ned Sawyer are the final two poignant character sketches in *Beyond Desire*, and Red is caught between them, the one unwittingly driving him forward to martyrdom, the other waiting with gun in hand but not one bit liking the role he has to play. The Anderson of romantic individualism here becomes Anderson the fatalistic naturalist with each of his characters playing a role determined by larger forces. In a sense that was the crux of Anderson's romanticism. He did believe that industrialism and finance capitalism created a world that robbed individuals of control over their own destiny, and he held on to the pastoral belief, false though it might be, that in a preindustrial world individuals' destinies were not so constrained.

Molly, the farm girl, still only twenty, has experienced unhappy love and has had to endure the change from her farm home to the mill and its machines, marked by "clatter, clatter. What a racket there is." Everything jerked: "you get the jerks" (286). In a very few pages Anderson again sketches in impressionistically a poignant figure, one for whom, however, Red will never quite be a real person and one for whom Anderson hardly posits an attractive future.

Ned Sawyer meanwhile is a promising young college graduate, now a soldier in command of his unit of the reserves called up to quell a possible riot. He damns communism but feels no enmity toward the mill workers. His sister Louise is actually a radical leftist. Like more than one Anderson character stuck in such a role, he considers himself a "silly ass" (350). When the leader of the strikers steps forward to challenge the reservists' mettle, someone pulls him back. Red, not even part of the group, steps forward and catches the fatal bullet. The strike fails; Red dies to no purpose; end of story. *Beyond Desire* is not a well built novel, but at times it is a moving one as this author who so united Emersonian individualism, Twain's skepticism, and Adams's world-weariness with an admiration for Dreiser creates his only tragic structure, one in which the hero dies violently, but builds it within a wall of forces and cynical nihilism that removes any significance from the hero's death and life and that leaves the heroine in a marriage as empty of meaning as the hero's death.

KIT BRANDON

Kit Brandon is the story of a resourceful and attractive mountain girl who flees a father she fears will molest her, works in a textile mill and shoe store, and then becomes a notorious but successful driver in a North Carolina moonshine operation run by one Tom Halsey, whose son Kit marries. The marriage is dysfunctional. The novel is told not by a third-person narrator but rather by an older man Kit has engaged to hear and write her story. He listens while she drives him around in a car. By that time she is nearly thirty.

It is not clear why Anderson does not return the focus to his unnamed narrator at the end of the book. In some ways, however, *Kit Brandon* is, in conception and execution, the best of Anderson's novels. One reason is that it revolves around perception of a character, not the growth of a character or social thematics, with which Anderson is less skillful. It revolves around the narrator's at times awestruck, at times more objective perception and portrayal of a remarkable woman. Unfortunately, toward the end the voice of the narrator as significant character recedes and the voice becomes that of a flatter authorial speaker. Although the book would fall short anyway of the major achievements of Fitzgerald and Faulkner, Anderson does thereby lose some of the resonance that they achieve by balancing at the end, for example, a reader's interest in Nick Carraway and Jay Gatsby, Quentin Compson and Thomas Sutpen. Kit Brandon, one infers, ends her work with Tom Halsey, escapes the law, and some time later, through a mutual contact, arranges for this writer to record and tell her story. Through much of the book her fascinating story is balanced against the narrator's amazed engagement with it, and as a result the reader, too, engages Kit's story through his mind and eyes. The mountain-girl/mill-worker/shop-clerk/bootleg-driver heroine develops as a mixture of the familiar and the exotic in no small part because of the narrative method. The ending is flat because the connection to the narrator as a character is lost. The story just ends. There is no final suggestion that the act of making sense of Kit and her story has been one purpose of the book.

Kit Brandon includes typical Anderson themes. Bootlegger Tom Halsey is portrayed as, in some ways, a representative American businessman, a portrayal allowing Anderson to attack contemporary business ethics and American myths about capitalism, but also to enrich his portrayal of Appalachian mountain men, a group he had come to admire, with reservations, since moving to Virginia. He also continues the theme that "perhaps women" will provide, in one way or another, the vitality and strength for the future of America. Kit is an outlaw, tough but not really cruel, but also the most positively presented of Anderson's fictional females.

Anderson features mountain people through the voice of a some-what amazed urban flatlander struggling to make a complete picture of this east Tennessee–born hill woman. The most memorable of her traits is not her physical appeal but her obsession with driving cars. Anderson draws an ironic connection between her hill roots and her attraction to the machine age, just as he does between Tom Halsey and the Rockefeller-Carnegie types of America. But the fascination of Kit, for narrator and reader, is tied to her cars and driving, right from the start when she tells her listener, "You let me drive." The role of driver, normally masculine in Anderson's America, never re-duces Kit's womanliness but does assert her potential dominance in any relationship. Although speed is a theme, control is the more common motif of Kit's love of cars and of the novel: who controls his own life on the mountain, in the mill, at the still?

This book allows Anderson to exploit his strength at the impres-sionistic sketch and short narrative, at the interpolated tale whose relevance gradually emerges. The stories of Kit's friends Agnes and Sarah; the sketches of two Virginia boys, Alfred and Joel; the tale of Ike Lawler and his family all have the resonance of the best sketches in *Winesburg, Ohio* and become important to *Kit Brandon*.

Yet Kit is always at the center of this book, maybe more than any other central character in an Anderson novel. By the end of the first chapter she has fled her hill beginnings—the slovenly dirty house, her indolent defeated mother, her taciturn father. But that first chapter also establishes the importance of the narrator, a journalist who is connected to Kit through a businesswoman he knows, and Kit wants her story told. At that time she is handsome, tall, slender, dark-haired, and a "curious American phenomenon," a tough woman who with her skills in a different place might "have been one of our successful ones, another Rockefeller, a Harriman, a Gould" (8).[3] The narrator affects a shock at what he learns because it is such a sur-prise. At the same time she wants her story told, moreover, he senses in her an ambivalence about having it told: "She was wanting to tell her story and not wanting" (32). In any case, the distinction is drawn that what follows is "knowledge" for her and a "story . . . for me." She has "her way of knowing, and it seemed to me more real than most of the ways of knowing most of us have" (2), but he is the fiction-maker, the storyteller, the writer. Some of the subtlety of the Kit-nar-rator relationship later evaporates as the narration becomes flatter, but for some time Anderson achieves significance out of contrasts between the time of Kit's work in the mill with her time as a driver and with the time of the narration.

The Greenville factory scenes are on the one hand of a piece with those in *Beyond Desire* but also crucial to the portrayal of Kit. Anderson suggests that this is not to be a union novel by the statement that the "labor movement . . . did not touch her" (54). On arrival she was "still the frightened little mountain girl" (59) awed by the strangeness and wonder of a mill town. Kit receives part of her education from Agnes, the strong, vital, red-haired, angry leader of workers who befriends her but finally has little in common with her. Agnes was in the violent Marion strike and even had to change her name afterward to escape the law. She would later be in the Gastonia strike. While Anderson offers a negative picture of mill owners, working conditions, and the world of factories, he still backs off from any commitment to union or class. He returns to his earlier validation of the individual, implying, as in *Beyond Desire*, that radicals may well allow workers to be killed if the cause is helped and suggesting that Americans too often "group people" in categories such as "capitalist" or "proletarian." What factories destroy are self-respect, vitality, and decency.

Kit has her first sexual experience with Frank, a young tubercular man, who dies soon afterward. She maintains a feminine nature (92) as if Anderson's point is to show a woman as heroine without being unsexed. Kit's desires are presented as suitable for postwar young women (103), and Anderson ties his themes closely to the period in which the story is set. In one of the stronger impressionistic sketches (104–8) the postwar world of autos, speed, and power is balanced against the different ways in which Kit and Agnes try to fulfill themselves.

To paraphrase Melville's Ishmael, a mill town is Kit's Harvard College and her Yale. Her other early mentor is Sarah, a blonde she meets during her shoe store years, scenes narrated long after the novel has taken Kit into Tom Halsey's world. Sarah teachers her how to exploit men and to use her sexuality. Kit never becomes, like Sarah, a sex-for-dollars practitioner, but always remains inner-directed as she navigates through Tom's world increasingly confident of her own strength. Much of the story focuses on the dynamic between Kit and Tom, the partnership and growing tension. She, Tom decides, is a suitable spouse for son Gordon, though, of course, Gordon is hardly as suitable of a son as Kit, if a male, would be. When the marriage fails and clearly will not yield a grandson, Kit offers to pull her weight instead as a driver, cars being her passion. When out of jealousy at her highly publicized and notorious success in his service, or out of suspicion that Kit is not fully loyal, Tom, or so Kit convinces herself, plans to do her in, she first decides to confront him. Then, during a federal raid, she flees. Tom and others are killed. Gordon is jailed. Although Kit had previously spent time in prison, she apparently is not arrested after that episode, the final scene in the novel.

While Kit is developed as a mountain heroine, Tom Halsey is drawn with some irony as a businessman. Anderson parodies the American "cult of the businessman" while portraying a mountain man as resourceful and talented and entrepreneurial. Finally he is a villain rather than a hero, perhaps, but only as today an Enron or Worldcom executive, after years of *Business Week* profiles of his success, may show up as a venal or shameless scoundrel. Anderson in his last years found Appalachian mountaineers to be fascinating figures. He reminds the reader that they are not one type but many types (115) and should not be overgeneralized. Chapter 5 includes an engaging essay on mountain men, interpolated as Faulkner might include an essay on the mule or the backwoods farmer in the middle of a narrative. The mountain men are America's forgotten, these Scotch-Irish antigovernment people with their moonshine, superstitions, and often terrible health. Neither the lumber kings who ravished the land nor the big land companies who cheated its people had in the end any real interest in the kind of poor soil that was home to these folk. Chapter 5 culminates in a "hymn" to mountain men and a lyrical assault on lumber companies.

Tom Halsey grows up in that world, as Kit herself does, and as in a sense Faulkner's Thomas Sutpen does in a novel published the same year as *Kit Brandon.* As the pre–Civil War Sutpen emulated successful plantation owners, so Halsey, Anderson suggests, in cornering a piece of the moonshine trade during Prohibition is of a piece with Harriman and Rockefeller and Carnegie. He is not as grand or as wealthy, to be sure, but the difference is one of degree not kind. One might remember that even Al Capone more than once called himself simply an American business executive responding to the needs of the market.

Anderson pulls back from sentimentalizing Halsey, partly by showing his cruel and venal and coarse sides and partly by portraying him at third remove, through both the narrator and Kit, who comes to learn his weaknesses as well as his strengths. The life of Tom Halsey, nonetheless, is a fascinating one that includes several engaging stories, stories of the sickly girl he rescues and later marries, of her death after giving birth to Gordon (stories Tom tells to Kit), of the woman Kate and her lover the preacher Joe Lawler whose cruel father Ike makes his sons rob henhouses but who nearly kills his own family, and of Tom taking Kate away from Joe in the middle of a camp meeting to nurse and mother his infant son. As always Anderson is at his best in such short narrative and impressionistic sketches, and as a result some of these central chapters are the most satisfying parts of the book. Kate remains a mystery, to the reader and pretty much to the narrator and Anderson as well. She speaks little, has been blindly loyal to Tom for years, has raised Gordon, and ends up in jail with him. Kit had come to feel that talking with Kate would improve her failing relationship with Tom, but that talk never takes place.

Meanwhile the narrator keeps puzzling over the relationship between Tom and Kit. Since his perspective is not ironically undercut, a reader is inclined to go through the same puzzling. Is Tom sexually attracted to Kit (213) or is respect the key to his positive feeling (214)? At the start they like each other, and Tom clearly has chosen her to play some role in his life (218). When the collapse of Gordon's marriage deprives Tom of his plans for a "dynasty," a grandson who will also have the respectability he cannot have (223, 335), Tom is open to Kit's offer to be a driver. From then on, however, she develops a fear of not, now, the father-in-law, but rather, in her new identity, her gangster-boss. His distrust of women generally, his exploitative nature, his greed (271, 278) come to dominate her picture of him. Meanwhile she becomes an expert on rural roads, studying them, as a hundred years earlier the best riverboat pilot on the Mississippi would have learned every bend in the river, so that she can escape any pursuing car at high speed. Lonely all her life (246), Kit creates her own romance with new clothes, shoes, aliases, and notoriety in the newspapers as "the rum-running queen" known to the police as "Kit Halsey." The dominant image of Kit in the book is of a lonely driver on dangerous mountain roads, a figure now older and telling her story as she drives, a hazy heroine rather than the actual mountain girl and mill worker she had once been. The novel to some extent depends on a tension between the "facts" of her story put together by the narrator and the almost mythic figure on "thunder road," who seems to the narrator more deeply significant and more heroic than Tom Halsey or maybe even than John D. Rockefeller.

Other than the fatal shooting of Halsey's disloyal partner, Steve Wyagle, the most memorable parts of the book's conclusion are two final sketches of young men. One is Alfred Weathersmythe, son of a mountain girl and a First Families of Virginia father. Hating his father, a hypocritical Prohibition political candidate and heavy drinker, but revering his grandfather, the Mosby-like mountain man, Alfred in rebellion joins Tom's gang and then is exploited by him to do the murder of Wyagle. He flees, with Kit's help, and she never sees him again. His successor for Kit is Joel Haneford, whose father is a Virginia judge and whose mountain-man grandfather was a Civil War deserter. Joel, wounded in World War I, is a physical wreck and always drunk, but Kit, attracted again and again to dependent men, says, "I'd like to take care of him." She likes "his bitter resistance" to his father and the establishment. It is not clear what happens to him because Kit ends up, as it were, like Huck Finn or Ken Kesey striking out on the road for some territory until found in South Dakota by the narrator.

If not fully realized, Kit is still Anderson's most engaging fictional character, partly because of the narrative method he uses, a method that creates fascination with Kit and participation in the process of putting the diverse pieces together to make a credible picture. It is the only time, except with the unpublished novels about May Edgely and Mary Cochran, when Anderson set out deliberately to create a central female character, although most of his novels have a strong female presence in a significant role. While the Anderson of *Perhaps Women* is a shallow thinker, in his fiction he was always striving to understand women as much as men.

Conclusion

Anderson did not publish another novel in his last five years. The rich collection of materials he was compiling for his *Memoirs*, however, indicate that up to the end he was still exploring and capturing the essence of the tension between on the one hand the many facts, episodes, and impressions he records and on the other this "Sherwood Anderson" who survives as the author of many books.

In some ways Anderson's career may best be reviewed by seeing *Winesburg, Ohio* and *Kit Brandon* as bookends. In each case Anderson develops a primary character as a listener-observer: in the first case, a bright young man who at least potentially might go off to tell tales about and make sense of the puzzled and puzzling villagers whom he has come to know; in the second case, a sadder and older man also telling a tale about and trying to make sense of a world strange and new to him. Anderson so well conveys the experience of the sensitive but at times baffled observer, as he can convey impressionistically the bafflement of the frustrated and lonely and uncommunicating individual in a world where the pieces just do not quite fit together.

Before his first fictional success Anderson tried out several narratives of the young man or woman striving for meaning, identity, and satisfaction, but he never quite figured out how to get beyond the opening act that defined the problem, the frustration, the hazy goal. After the accomplishment of *Winesburg, Ohio* and the more flawed but somewhat paired accomplishment of *Poor White*, Anderson—even while penning numerous fine short pieces—again resorted to trying out narratives of the middle-aged man striving for liberation and a new life in midstream, but again he never quite solved the problem of developing a credible and satisfying outcome after defining his character's problem. At times it has seemed to me that the manuscript with the greatest potential for excellence during this period of his life was the story of May Edgely in "Ohio Pagans," a story that might well have conveyed the frustrations of adult life had Anderson developed for it an outside narrator-observer like the one in *Kit Brandon.* But during the 1920s he often had trouble going beyond his self-explorations whether in novels or in his several autobiographical works, and the writing is stronger when it is deliberately—even if at times fictively—autobiographical, as in *A Story Teller's Story* and *Sherwood Anderson's Notebook.*

He moved beyond this phase when he turned to nonfiction and social criticism; and while his generalizations about mountaineers and women are of limited value his essays capture episode and impression as richly as his tales of Winesburg do. The final novels in retrospect seem a paired set of recapitulations to a writer's career. The first revisits the paradigm of a baffled youth lost in seeking his identity and his future and ends more cynically and tragically than any earlier Anderson novel; the other reasserts the value of the writer as the one who listens and observes and captures the essence of the lives around him. Both are products of the 1930s, not the 1910s or 1920s, but both are also clearly the work of that same midwestern Emersonian, one might say, learning the sad truth that the "real self" is not something achieved at a glorious end but something lived along the highway and, for the writer, observed and valued and communicated to others in such a way as to make all of us a little more aware of the lives of others. His best work does continue to make the alert and sensitive reader a bit more aware of the feelings and strivings and frustrations of those "others" among whom we all live.

Notes

PREFACE

1. The best recent approach to the whole issue of regionalism is Robert L. Dorman, *Revolt of the Provinces: The Regionalist Movement in America, 1920–1945* (Chapel Hill: University of North Carolina Press, 1993). The still indispensable study of American literary nationalism is Benjamin Townley Spencer, *The Quest for Nationality; An American Literary Campaign* (Syracuse: Syracuse University Press, 1957).

2. Robert Dunne offers cogent criticisms of White's edition in "The Book of the Grotesque: Textual Theory and the Editing of *Winesburg, Ohio*," *Studies in Short Fiction* 35, no. 3 (Summer 1998): 287–96.

1. AN OHIO PAGAN

1. Scholars and general readers of Anderson's work have for some time been eagerly awaiting publication of Walter B. Rideout's comprehensive biography of the author. Until it appears, the standard biography is Kim Townsend's *Sherwood Anderson* (Boston: Houghton Mifflin, 1987). I am indebted to it but also to William A. Sutton, *The Road to Winesburg* (Metuchen, N.J.: Scarecrow, 1972) and Kenny J. Williams, *A Storyteller and a City: Sherwood Anderson's Chicago* (DeKalb: Northern Illinois University Press, 1988), as well as to the collections of letters and diaries listed in the Selected Bibliography and dozens of articles by David D. Anderson, Rideout, Hilbert H. Campbell, and Ray Lewis White on various parts of Anderson's life. The earlier items are well summarized by Rideout in his excellent bibliographical essay in *Sixteen Modern American Authors* (New York: Norton, 1973). The other starting point for any research on Anderson is White's *Sherwood Anderson: A Reference Guide* (Boston: G. K. Hall, 1977).

2. Marc Conner offers the richest recent exploration of the way Anderson's enmity toward his father plays itself out in the writing. See "Fathers and Sons: *Winesburg, Ohio* and the Revision of Modernism," *Studies in American Fiction* 29, no. 2 (Autumn 2001): 209–38

3. Useful and insightful on the year at Wittenberg is William Baker's article, "Sherwood Anderson in Springfield," *American Literary Realism 1870–1910* 15, no. 1 (Spring 1982): 47–61.

4. Charles E. Modlin, ed., *Sherwood Anderson: Selected Letters* (Knoxville: University of Tennessee Press, 1984), 20.

5. See Chapter 2 of Anderson's *Sherwood Anderson: An Introduction and Interpretation* (New York: Holt, Rinehart, 1967).

6. The correspondence between them is collected in *Sherwood Anderson/Gertrude Stein: Correspondence and Personal Essays*, ed. Ray Lewis White (Chapel Hill: University of North Carolina Press, 1972).

7. On another unfinished work, a handful of pages in an epistolary form, see Charles E. Modlin, "The Education of Sidney Adams: Anderson's 'Letters to Cynthia,'" *Sherwood Anderson Review* 25, no. 2 (2000): 5–11.

8. White, ed., *Sherwood Anderson*, 314–15.

2. A New Profession

1. Sherwood Anderson, *Windy McPherson's Son* (New York and London: John Lane, 1916). This is the text for all passages except one taken from the revised edition (note 2).

2. Sherwood Anderson, *Windy McPherson's Son*, rev. ed. (New York: B. W. Huebsch, 1922), 324.

3. Several critics have dealt sympathetically and insightfully with this first novel. Of particular note are J. R. Scafidel, "Sexuality in *Windy McPherson's* Son," *Twentieth Century Literature* 23 (February 1977): 94–101; and Carl Smith in *Chicago and the American Literary Imagination, 1880–1920* (Chicago: University of Chicago Press, 1984).

4. Wiliam A. Sutton, ed., *Letters to Bab: Sherwood Anderson to Marietta D. Finley, 1916–33* (Urbana: University of Illinois Press, 1985), 69. In a footnote to this letter Sutton reprints "From Chicago," Anderson's essay on writing that appeared in the May 1917 issue of *Seven Arts*. The essay is noteworthy because, as Sutton says (70), in it Anderson also indicates how he "dramatized a portion of himself in *Marching Men*."

5. Mark Whalen, "Dreams of Manhood: Narrative, Gender, and History in *Winesburg, Ohio*," *Studies in American Fiction* 30, no. 2 (2002): 229–48. Also see an earlier article by John Ditsky, "Sherwood Anderson's *Marching Men:* Unnatural Disorder and the Art of Force," *Twentieth Century Literature* 23, no. 1 (1977): 102–14. Ditsky says that "it is hard to agree with the notion that Anderson clearly rejects the lock-step totalitarianism he portrays so prophetically."

6. Sherwood Anderson, *Marching Men* (New York and London: John Lane, 1917). This is the text used for all passages. Ray Lewis White edited "a critical text" in 1972 in the Case Western Reserve University edition.

7. The only readily available text for "Mary Cochran" is "An Edition of Sherwood Anderson's *Mary Cochran*," the dissertation of William S. Pfeiffer (Kent State University, 1975). All quotations are based on that work. See Pfeiffer's fine article on the manuscript, "*Mary Cochran*: Sherwood Anderson's Ten-Year Novel," *Studies in Bibliography* 31 (1978): 248–57.

8. See Walter B. Rideout, "Talbott Whittingham and Anderson: A Passage to *Winesburg, Ohio*," in *Sherwood Anderson: Dimensions of His Literary Art*, ed. David D.

Anderson (East Lansing: Michigan State University Press, 1976), 41–60. The "Talbott Whittingham" material is in the Newberry Collection W49(6) through W50(5).

9. This particular passage comes from chapter 4 of the manuscript.

10. Sherwood Anderson, *Mid-American Chants* (New York and London: John Lane, 1918).

11. Sutton, *Letters to Bab*, 85.

12. Sherwood Anderson, *A New Testament* (New York: Boni & Liveright, 1927).

3. LITERARY SUCCESS

1. Ray Lewis White, ed., *Sherwood Anderson's* Winesburg, Ohio *with Variant Readings and Annotations* (Athens: Ohio University Press, 1997). This text is the source for all quotations. White also edited the now standard classroom edition for Norton, published in 1996.

2. "The New Note" appeared in *Little Review* in March 1914, "More About the New Note" in April 1914. "Sister" appeared there in December 1915 and "The Story Writers" in *Smart Set* in January 1916. All these plus other early pieces are included in White's *Sherwood Anderson's Early Writings* (Kent: Kent State University Press, 1989).

3. The story of Anderson's relationship with Ben Huebsch is best covered in Catherine McCullough's dissertation, "A History of B. W. Huebsch, Publisher" (PhD diss., University of Wisconsin, 1979).

4. Benjamin Townley Spencer, "Sherwood Anderson: American Mythopoeist," *American Literature* 41, no. 1 (March 1969): 126–44.

5. David D. Anderson has frequently made this point as, for example, in Chapter 3 of *Sherwood Anderson: An Introduction and Interpretation*. Also see Barry Gross, "The Revolt That Wasn't: The Legacies of Critical Myopia," *CEA Critic* 39, no. 2 (January 1977): 4–8.

6. Clarence Lindsay, " 'I Belong in Little Towns': Sherwood Anderson's Small Town Postmodernism," *Midamerica* 26 (1999): 77–104. Also see his, "Another Look at Community in *Winesburg, Ohio*," *Midamerica* 20 (1993): 76–88. Lindsay sees a sense of community as "interpreter of the fictions of selfhood" as crucial to the book.

7. Sutton, *Letters to Bab*, 15.

8. Marc Conner, "Fathers and Sons: *Winesburg, Ohio* and the Revision of Modernism." Conner describes the first traumatic scene between David and Jesse as expressing "the terrifying demon that lurks behind the father-figure throughout the *Winesburg* stories" (213).

9. Chris Browning, "Pedagogy of the Undressed: Sherwood Anderson's Kate Swift, "*Studies in Short Fiction* 36 (1999): 361–68. Browning's argument is in "Kate Swift: Sherwood Anderson's Creative Eros," *Tennessee Studies in Literature* 8 (1968): 141–48.

10. Mark Whalen argues strongly that World War I was a powerful influence on Anderson and this book and ties it to "a crisis in his gendered views about narrative." He says that the "tyrannical and even absurd nature of the desire for control through art is pushed to the forefront" in this book, which emphasizes "the absolute masculinism" that George struggles "to achieve throughout the cycle." Some

of Whalen's most provocative comments focus on similarities he perceives between George and Beaut McGregor and on the "appropriation" of Kate Swift's
body by both Hartman and George. See "Dreams of Manhood: Narrative, Gender,
and History in *Winesburg, Ohio.*"

11. The words of Emerson appear in "Experience," an essay from 1844. See *Essays: Second Series* (Boston: James Munroe, 1844), 68.

12. Marcia Jacobson, "*Winesburg, Ohio* and the Autobiographical Moment," in
New Essays on Winesburg, Ohio, ed. John W. Crowley (Cambridge: Cambridge
University Press, 1990): 53–72.

13. Sherwood Anderson, *Poor White* (New York: B. W. Huebsch, 1920). One useful and often cited item on this novel is an interview Eleanor Copenhaver did with
Anderson in 1931. It is included in *Sherwood Anderson: Centennial Studies*, ed.
Hilbert H. Campbell and Charles E. Modlin (Troy, N.Y.: Whitston, 1976). In a letter to Huebsch Anderson said the new novel "is really the story of the development of an American town into an industrial center and the effect of the coming
of industrials on the people." Modlin, *Sherwood Anderson: Selected Letters*, 18.

14. Arguments about Anderson's portrayal of women seem to derive more
from critics' own predispositions than from the texts themselves. There is plenty
of material to justify a case for Anderson being conservative, unenlightened, and
biased in relation to women or a case for him being ahead of other male writers in
seeking to explore seriously the challenges and tensions experienced by American
women. He is not a writer whose work has attracted the attention of many critics
strongly influenced by Continental feminism, but the range of views is broad.
Some critics like William V. Miller argue that Anderson's females are limited in
their development and narrowly portrayed, or like Marilyn Atlas that he creates no
woman with the potential to change her future, or like Clare Colquitt that he
never allows women to escape their situations. Other critics like Nancy Bunge and
Sally Rigsbee have been more tolerant and sympathetic to Anderson's often baffled efforts to "understand" his own female characters. All the above items are
listed in the Selected Bibliography.

4. THE SHORT STORIES

1. Valuable for any scholarship on the stories is Judy Jo Small, *A Reader's Guide
to the Short Stories of Sherwood Anderson* (Boston: G. K. Hall, 1994). It does not cover
uncollected stories but has essential information on composition, publication,
and criticism of the stories in *Winesburg, Ohio, The Triumph of the Egg, Horses and
Men,* and *Death in the Woods and Other Stories.*

2. Sherwood Anderson, *The Triumph of the Egg* (New York: B. W. Huebsch,
1921).

3. A useful recent study is Tom Hansen, "Who's a Fool? A Rereading of Sherwood Anderson's 'I'm a Fool,'" *Midwest Quarterly* 38, no. 3 (1997): 372–79.

4. Rex Burbank, chapter 5 of *Sherwood Anderson* (New York: Twayne, 1964).

5. William A. Sutton's study of the process of revising "Seeds" is especially instructive about Anderson's habits of composition and revision. See *The Revision of
"Seeds,"* Ball State University Studies (Muncie, Ind.: Ball State University Press, 1976).

6. Sherwood Anderson, *Horses and Men* (New York: B. W. Huebsch, 1923).

7. Clare Colquitt, "The Reader as Voyeur: Complicitous Transformations in 'Death in the Woods,' " *Modern Fiction Studies* 32, no. 2 (Summer 1986): 175–90.

8. Mary Anne Feruson, "Sherwood Anderson's *Death in the Woods*: Toward a New Realism," *Midamerica* 7 (1980): 173–95. For a more recent assessment of the relationship between the woman and the narrator see William V. Miller, "Texts, Subtexts and More Texts: Reconstructing the Narrator's Role in Sherwood Anderson's 'Death in the Woods,' " in *Exploring the Midwestern Literary Imagination*, ed. Marcie Noe (Troy, N.Y.: Whitston, 1993), 86–98.

9. Jon Lawry, " 'Death in the Woods' and the Artist's Self in Sherwood Anderson," *PMLA* 74 (June 1959): 306–11.

10. Sherwood Anderson, *Death in the Woods and Other Stories* (New York: Horace Liveright, 1933).

11. For some time William V. Miller planned to bring out a comprehensive edition of Anderson's seventy-eight stories, but it has not appeared.

12. There is a great deal of commentary on Anderson's stories and his techniques in the short story. One of the best essays is Frank Gado's introduction to *The Teller's Tales: Short Stories by Sherwood Anderson* (Schenectady, N.Y.: Union College Press, 1983).

5. NOVELS OF MIDLIFE CRISIS

1. Sutton, *Letters to Bab*, 144, 146. Lawrence, by the way, liked *Many Marriages* but not *Dark Laughter*. See Kim Townsend, *Sherwood Anderson*, 227.

2. Sutton, *Letters to Bab*, 176.

3. Modlin, *Sherwood Anderson: Selected Letters*, 32.

4. Howard M. Jones and Walter B. Rideout, eds., *Letters of Sherwood Anderson* (Boston: Little, Brown, 1953), 338; 380.

5. Sherwood Anderson, *Many Marriages* (New York: B. W. Huebsch, 1923).

6. The foreword is not paginated.

7. Sutton, *Letters to Bab*, 139.

8. Jones and Rideout, *Letters of Sherwood Anderson*, 58.

9. Sherwood Anderson, *Dark Laughter* (New York: Boni & Liveright, 1925).

10. On this topic see Mark Helbling, "Sherwood Anderson and Jean Toomer," *Negro American Literature Forum* 9, no. 2 (Summer 1975): 35–39; Mary Jane Dickerson, "Sherwood Anderson and Jean Toomer: A Literary Relationship, " *Studies in American Fiction* 1, no. 1 (Autumn 1973): 163–65; Darwin T. Turner, "An Intersection of Paths: Correspondence Between Jean Toomer and Sherwood Anderson," *College Language Association Journal* 17, no. 4 (June 1974): 455–67; and Charles Scruggs, "The Reluctant Witness: What Jean Toomer Remembered from *Winesburg, Ohio*," *Studies in American Fiction* 28, no. 1 (Spring 2000): 77–100.

11. On the influence of Anderson's New Orleans experiences on his writing see Walter B. Rideout, " 'The Most Cultural Town in America': Sherwood Anderson and New Orleans," *Southern Review* 24, no. 1 (Winter 1988): 79–99.

12. Helpful to understanding Anderson's view of Paris is Michael Fanning's *France and Sherwood Anderson: Paris Notebook, 1921* (Baton Rouge: Louisiana State

University Press, 1976). This includes Anderson's own notes on his Paris trip and a study by Fanning.

13. Newberry Collection W15 (22). Of related interest is a manuscript story "Farmer Swartz & Agnes," a tale of a German farmer who tries to take sexually a young worker on his farm. Newberry Collection W16 (20).

14. Newberry Collection W40 (4) through W40 (6).

6. THE NONFICTION

1. *Sherwood Anderson's Notebook* (1926; Mamaroneck, N.Y.: Paul P. Appel, 1970).

2. *The Modern Writer* was published in San Francisco by Gelber, Lilienthal in 1925. It is reprinted in *Homage to Sherwood Anderson: 1876–1941*, ed. Paul P. Appel (Mamaroneck, N.Y.: Paul P. Appel, 1970), 173–90.

3. Sutton, *Letters to Bab*, 29–30.

4. Sherwood Anderson, *Hello Towns!* (New York: Horace Liveright, 1929).

5. Welford Dunaway Taylor, ed., *Sherwood Anderson: The Buck Fever Papers* (Charlottesville; University Press of Virginia, 1971); Ray Lewis White, ed., *Return to Winesburg* (Chapel Hill: University of North Carolina Press, 1967).

6. In addition to Taylor's fine introduction, another thoughtful early piece on Buck Fever is Walter B. Rideout, "Why Sherwood Anderson Employed Buck Fever," *Georgia Review* 13, no. 1 (Spring 1959): 76–85. Also see Leland Krauth, "Sherwood Anderson's Buck Fever; Or, Frontier Humor Comes to Town," *Studies in American Humor* 3, no. 4 (Winter 1984–85): 298–308. On *Hello Towns!* see David D. Anderson, "Sherwood Anderson, Virginia Journalist," *Newberry Library Bulletin* 6 (July 1971): 251–62.

7. Newberry Collection W29 (10).

8. Sherwood Anderson, *Perhaps Women* (New York: Horace Liveright, 1931).

9. Sherwood Anderson, *Puzzled America* (New York and London: Charles Scribner's Sons, 1935). Providing a useful context for Anderson's late writings and ideas on politics is Hilbert H. Campbell's "Selections from the Diary of Eleanor Anderson, 1933–40," *Sherwood Anderson Review* 26, no. 1 (2001): 1–76.

10. An earlier version of this essay was published in a limited edition as part of *Nearer the Grass Roots [and] Elizabethton* (San Francisco: Westgate Press, 1929).

11. Sherwood Anderson, *No Swank* (Philadelphia: Centaur Press, 1934).

12. "Brown Bomber" is reprinted in *The Sherwood Anderson Reader*, ed. Paul Rosenfeld (Boston: Houghton Mifflin, 1947), 679–85.

13. The other book published in this period was a collection of plays, *Winesburg and Others* (1937). While writing for the theater was not a major part of Anderson's accomplishment, he did put some effort into designing works for the stage. The book includes a stage version of *Winesburg*, performed at Hedgerow Theater in Media, Pennsylvania; "Triumph of the Egg" done in Provincetown, Massachusetts; "Mother" produced at Johns Hopkins University in Baltimore, Maryland; and "They Married Later," not produced. The Newberry Collection includes numerous other short plays in manuscript including "Tobacco Market," "Textiles," and "Man Has Hands." Also see note 9 to chapter 7.

7. AUTOBIOGRAPHIES

1. Martha Mulroy Curry edited *The "Writer's Book" by Sherwood Anderson: A Critical Edition* (Metuchen, N.J.: Scarecrow, 1975).

2. "The Education of Sherwood Anderson," in *Sherwood Anderson: Centennial Studies*, ed. Hilbert H. Campbell and Charles E. Modlin (Troy, N.Y.: Whitston, 1976) 185–201. Also see Thomas Cooley, *Educated Lives: The Rise of Modern Autobiography in America* (Columbus: Ohio State University Press, 1976), 138–56.

3. Sherwood Anderson, *A Story-Teller's Story* (New York: B. W. Huebsch, 1924). This passage comes from the book's subtitle.

4. For a study of the ways Anderson validated myths about his life, see Timothy Dow Adams, *Telling Lies in Autobiography* (Chapel Hill: University of North Carolina Press, 1990), 39–68. On family facts one always wants to check William A. Sutton, *The Road to Winesburg* (Metuchen, N.J.: Scarecrow Press, 1972).

5. A thoughtful recent article on changes in Anderson's treatment of the father after *Windy McPherson's Son* is Paul W. Miller, "Sherwood Anderson's Discovery of a Father," *Midamerica* 26 (1999): 113–20. Also essential reading is Marc Conner's article, "Fathers and Sons: *Winesburg, Ohio* and the Revision of Modernism."

6. Sherwood Anderson, *Tar: A Midwest Childhood* (1926; Cleveland: The Press of Case Western Reserve University, 1969). This edition was edited by Ray Lewis White. It includes "The Diaries of Sherwood Anderson's Parents" by William Alfred Sutton, an essay on diaries kept by Irwin and Emma Anderson. It also includes "The Death in the Forest," edited by William V. Miller. This is a twenty-two-page holograph early version of "Death in the Woods."

7. Ray Lewis White, ed., *Sherwood Anderson's Memoirs: A Critical Edition* (Chapel Hill: University of North Carolina Press, 1969).

8. Walter B. Rideout wrote a splendid review, "The Sherwood Anderson Story," *Virginia Quarterly Review* 45 (1969): 537-40.

9. As one considers Anderson's later reflections on the development of his career, it is striking to come across the unpublished fictional manuscript about "Fred Coleman," apparently drafted after 1939 because of an internal reference to Hitler taking Paris. Coleman is a Missouri boy who, when his parents die, is taken in by a wealthy uncle in Chicago, an attorney who sends him through law school. Fred, however, gains success as a playwright, and the unfinished tale goes on to explore his agonies over his career, success and artistry, sexual relations, and power. It also describes mingling with the Algonquin Hotel crowd and other New York literati. Newberry Collection W17 (4).

8. FINAL NOVELS

1. Sherwood Anderson, *Beyond Desire* (New York: Horace Liveright, 1932).

2. David D. Anderson has recently come out very positively on the way this novel represents labor unrest in the South. See "Sherwood Anderson's Midwest and the Industrial South in *Beyond Desire*," *Midamerica* 26 (1999): 105–12. Also of interest in this regard is an unfinished tale in manuscript with the heading, "They

wanted their jobs: The tale of a union meeting down south." In it Anderson is clearly seeking a sympathetic portrayal of textile workers but not of outside labor organizers. Newberry Collection W52 (13).

3. Sherwood Anderson, *Kit Brandon* (New York and London: Charles Scribner's Sons, 1936). Connections between this novel and the oral tradition were discussed years ago by Philip A. Greasley in "Sherwood Anderson's *Kit Brandon*: A Study in Oral Form," *Great Lakes Review* 5, no. 1 (1978): 42–48, and later in "Sherwood Anderson's Oral Tradition," *Midwestern Miscellany* 22 (1995): 9–16.

Selected Bibliography

PRIMARY MATERIALS

Books by Sherwood Anderson

Windy McPherson's Son. New York and London: John Lane, 1916; revised edition, New York: B. W. Huebsch, 1922; London: Jonathan Cape, 1923.

Marching Men. New York and London: John Lane, 1917.

Mid-American Chants. New York and London: John Lane, 1918.

Winesburg, Ohio. New York: B. W. Huebsch, 1919; London: Jonathan Cape, 1922.

Poor White. New York: B. W. Huebsch, 1920; London: Jonathan Cape, 1921.

The Triumph of the Egg. New York: B. W. Huebsch, 1921; London: Jonathan Cape, 1922.

Horses and Men. New York: B. W. Huebsch, 1923; London: Jonathan Cape, 1924.

Many Marriages. New York: B. W. Huebsch, 1923.

A Story-Teller's Story. New York: B. W. Huebsch, 1924; London: Jonathan Cape, 1925.

Dark Laughter. New York: Boni & Liveright, 1925; London: Jarrolds, 1926.

Sherwood Anderson's Notebook. New York: Boni & Liveright, 1926.

Tar: A Midwest Childhood. New York: Boni & Liveright, 1926; London: Secker, 1927.

A New Testament. New York: Boni & Liveright, 1927.

Hello Towns! New York: Horace Liveright, 1929.

Perhaps Women. New York: Horace Liveright, 1931.

Beyond Desire. New York: Horace Liveright, 1932.

Death in the Woods and Other Stories. New York: Horace Liveright, 1933.

No Swank. Philadelphia: Centaur Press, 1934.

Puzzled America. New York and London: Charles Scribner's Sons, 1935.

Kit Brandon. New York and London: Charles Scribner's Sons, 1936; London: Hutchinson, 1937.

Plays: Winesburg and Others. New York and London: Charles Scribner's Sons, 1937.

Home Town. New York: Alliance Book Corporation, 1940.

Sherwood Anderson's Memoirs. New York: Harcourt Brace, 1942.

Anderson's Letters and Diaries

Letters of Sherwood Anderson, edited by Howard Mumford Jones in association with Walter B. Rideout. Boston: Little, Brown, 1953.

Sherwood Anderson/Gertrude Stein: Correspondence and Personal Essays, edited by Ray Lewis White. Chapel Hill: University of North Carolina Press, 1972.

France and Sherwood Anderson: Paris Notebook, 1921, edited by Michael Fanning. Baton Rouge: Louisiana State University Press, 1976.

Letters to Bab: Sherwood Anderson to Marietta D. Finley, 1916–33, edited by William A. Sutton. Urbana: University of Illinois Press, 1985.

Selected Letters of Sherwood Anderson, edited by Charles E. Modlin. Knoxville: University of Tennessee Press, 1984.

The Sherwood Anderson Diaries, 1936–1941, edited by Hilbert H. Campbell. Athens: University of Georgia Press, 1987.

Sherwood Anderson's Love Letters to Eleanor Copenhaver Anderson, edited by Charles E. Modlin. Athens: University of Georgia Press, 1989.

Collections of Anderson's Works

The Sherwood Anderson Reader, edited by Paul Rosenfeld. Boston: Houghton Mifflin, 1947.

Sherwood Anderson: Short Stories, edited by Maxwell Geismar. New York: Hill and Wang, 1962.

Sherwood Anderson's Memoirs: A Critical Edition, edited by Ray Lewis White. Chapel Hill: University of North Carolina Press, 1969.

The Buck Fever Papers, edited by Welford Dunaway Taylor. Charlottesville: University of Virginia Press, 1971.

The "Writer's Book" by Sherwood Anderson: A Critical Edition, edited by Martha Mulroy Curry. Metuchen, N.J.: Scarecrow Press, 1975.

Sherwood Anderson: The Writer at His Craft, edited by Jack Salzman, David D. Anderson, and Kichinossuke Ohashi. Mamaroneck, N.Y.: Appel, 1979. Sixty-nine early pieces by Anderson.

The Teller's Tales: Short Stories by Sherwood Anderson, edited by Frank Gado. Schenectady, N.Y.: Union College Press, 1983.

Sherwood Anderson: Early Writings, edited by Ray Lewis White. Kent, OH: Kent State University Press, 1989.

Certain Things Last: The Selected Short Stories of Sherwood Anderson, edited by Charles E. Modlin. New York: Four Walls Eight Windows, 1992.

SECONDARY MATERIALS

Books about Anderson

Anderson, David D. *Sherwood Anderson: An Introduction and Interpretation.* New York: Holt, Rinehart, 1967.

Burbank, Rex. *Sherwood Anderson.* New York: Twayne Publishers, 1964.

Howe, Irving. *Sherwood Anderson.* New York: Sloane, 1951.

Papinchak, Robert Allen. *Sherwood Anderson: A Study of the Short Fiction.* New York: Twayne Publishers, 1992.

Schevill, James. *Sherwood Anderson: His Life and Work.* Denver, Colo.: University of Denver Press, 1951.

Small, Judy Jo. *A Reader's Guide to the Short Stories of Sherwood Anderson.* Boston: G. K. Hall, 1994.

Sutton, William A. *The Road to Winesburg: A Mosaic of the Imaginative Life of Sherwood Anderson.* Metuchen, N.J.: Scarecrow Press, 1972.

Taylor, Welford Dunaway. *Sherwood Anderson.* New York: Ungar, 1977.

Townsend, Kim. *Sherwood Anderson.* Boston: Houghton Mifflin, 1987.

White, Ray Lewis. *Sherwood Anderson: A Reference Guide.* Boston: G. K. Hall, 1977.

———. *Winesburg, Ohio: An Exploration.* Boston: Twayne Publishers, 1990.

Williams, Kenny J. *A Storyteller and a City: Sherwood Anderson's Chicago.* DeKalb: Northern Illinois University Press, 1988.

Collections of Essays and Articles about Anderson

Anderson, David D., ed. *Critical Essays on Sherwood Anderson.* Boston: G. K. Hall, 1981.

———, ed. *Sherwood Anderson: Dimensions of His Literary Art.* East Lansing: Michigan State University Press, 1976.

Appel, Paul P., ed. *Homage to Sherwood Anderson: 1876–1941.* Mamaroneck, N.Y.: Paul P. Appel, 1970.

Campbell, Hilbert H., and Charles E. Modlin, eds. *Sherwood Anderson: Centennial Studies.* Troy, N.Y.: Whitston Publishing, 1976. This also includes forty-four Anderson letters.

Crowley, John W., ed. *New Essays on* Winesburg, Ohio. Cambridge: Cambridge University Press, 1990.

Rideout, Walter B., ed. *Sherwood Anderson: A Collection of Critical Essays.* Englewood Cliffs, N.J.: Prentice-Hall, 1974.

White, Ray Lewis, comp. *The Merrill Studies in* Winesburg, Ohio. Columbus, Ohio: Charles E. Merrill, 1971.

———, ed. *Sherwood Anderson: Essays in Criticism.* Chapel Hill: University of North Carolina Press, 1966.

SELECTED ARTICLES
AND SECTIONS OF BOOKS

Adams, Timothy Dow. "Sherwood Anderson: 'Lies My Father Told Me.'" *Telling Lies in Modern American Autobiography.* Chapel Hill: University of North Carolina Press, 1990. 39–68.

Anderson, David D. "Sherwood Anderson, Virginia Journalist." *Newberry Library Bulletin* 6 (July 1971): 251–62.

———. "Sherwood Anderson and Myth." In *Sherwood Anderson: Dimensions of His Literary Art,* ed. Anderson. 118–41.

———. "Sherwood Anderson, Chicago, and the Midwestern Myth." *Midamerica* 11 (1984): 56–68.

———. "Sherwood Anderson's *Poor White* and the Grotesques Become Myth." *Midamerica* 14 (1987): 89–100.

———. "Sherwood Anderson's Midwest and the Industrial South in *Beyond Desire.*" *Midamerica* 26 (1999): 105–12.

Atlas, Marilyn Judith. "Sherwood Anderson and the Women of Winesburg." In *Critical Essays on Sherwood Anderson,* ed. Anderson. 250–66.

Baker, Carlos. "Sherwood Anderson's Winesburg: A Reprise." *Virginia Quarterly Review* 48, no.4 (Autumn 1972): 568–79.

Baker, William. "Sherwood Anderson in Springfield, "*American Literary Realism 1870–1910* 15, no. 1 (Spring 1982): 47–61.

Bidney, Martin. "Thinking about Walt and Melville in a Sherwood Anderson Tale: An Independent Woman's Transcendental Quest." *Studies in Short Fiction* 29, no. 4 (Fall 1992): 517–30.

Bunge, Nancy L. "The Ambiguous Endings of Sherwood Anderson's Novels." In *Sherwood Anderson: Centennial Studies,* ed. Campbell and Modlin. 249–63.

———. "Women in Sherwood Anderson's Fiction." In *Critical Essays on Sherwood Anderson,* ed. Anderson. 242–49.

Campbell, Hilbert H. "Selections from the Diary of Eleanor Anderson, 1933–40," *Sherwood Anderson Review* 26, no. 1 (2001): 1–76.

Ciancio, Ralph. " 'The Sweetness of the Twisted Apples': Unity of Vision in *Winesburg, Ohio.*" *PMLA* 87, iv (October 1972): 994–1006.

Colquitt, Claire. "The Reader as Voyeur: Complicitous Transformations in 'Death in the Woods.' " *Modern Fiction Studies* 32, no. 2 (Summer 1986): 175–90.

———. "Motherlove in the Narratives of Community: *Winesburg, Ohio* and *The Country of the Pointed Firs.*" In *New Essays* on Winesburg, Ohio, ed. Crowley. 73–92.

Conner, Marc C. "Fathers and Sons: *Winesburg, Ohio* and the Revision of Modernism." *Studies in American Fiction* 29, no. 2 (Autumn 2001): 209–38.

Cooley, Thomas. "Then as Now: Sherwood Anderson." *Educated Lives: The Rise of Modern Autobiography in America.* Columbus: Ohio State University Press, 1976. 138–56.

Crowley, John W. "The Education of Sherwood Anderson." In *Sherwood Anderson: Centennial Studies,* ed. Campbell and Modlin. 185–201.

Curry, Martha Mulroy. "Anderson's Theories on Writing Fiction." In *Sherwood Anderson: Dimensions of His Literary Art,* ed. Anderson. 90–109.

Dewey, Joseph. "No God in the Sky and No God in Myself: 'Godliness' and Anderson's *Winesburg.*" *Modern Fiction Studies* 35, no. 2 (Summer 1989): 251–59.

Dickerson, Mary Jane. "Sherwood Anderson and Jean Toomer: A Literary Relationship." *Studies in American Fiction* 1, no. 2 (Autumn 1973): 163–75.

Ditsky, John. "Sherwood Anderson's *Marching Men*: Unnatural Disorder and the Art of Force." *Twentieth Century Literature* 23, no. 1 (February 1977): 102–14.

Dunne, Robert. "The Book of the Grotesque: Textual Theory and the Editing of *Winesburg, Ohio.*" *Studies in Short Fiction* 35, no. 3 (Summer 1998): 287–96.

Ferguson, Mary Anne. "Sherwood Anderson's *Death in the Woods*: Toward a New Realism." *Midamerica* 7 (1980): 73–95.

Fludernik, Monica. "'The Divine Accident of Life': Metaphoric Structure and Meaning in *Winesburg, Ohio.*" *Style* 22, no. 1 (Spring 1988): 116–35.

———. "*Winesburg, Ohio*: The Apprenticeship of George Willard." *Amerikastudien* 32 (1987): 431–52.

Fussell, Edwin, "*Winesburg, Ohio*: Art and Isolation." *Modern Fiction Studies* 6, no. 1 (Spring 1960): 106–14.

———. "Sherwood Anderson's Oral Tradition." *Midwestern Miscellany* 22 (1995): 9–16.

Greasley, Philip A. "Sherwood Anderson's *Kit Brandon*: A Study in Oral Form." *Great Lakes Review*, 5, no. 1 (1978): 42–48.

Gross, Barry. "The Revolt That Wasn't: The Legacies of Critical Myopia." *CEA Critic* 39, no. 2 (January 1977): 4–8.

Hansen, Tom. "Who's a Fool? A Rereading of Sherwood Anderson's 'I'm a Fool.'" *Midwest Quarterly* 38, no. 3 (1997): 372–79.

Helbling, Mark. "Sherwood Anderson and Jean Toomer." *Negro American Literature Forum* 9, no. 2 (Summer 1975): 35–39.

Ingram, Forrest L. "Sherwood Anderson's *Winesburg, Ohio.*" *Representative Short Story Cycles of the Twentieth Century: Studies in a Literary Genre.* The Hague: Mouton, 1971. 143–99.

Jacobson, Marcia. "*Winesburg, Ohio* and the Autobiographical Moment." In *New Essays on* Winesburg, Ohio, ed. Crowley. 53–72.

Krauth, Leland. "Sherwood Anderson's Buck Fever; Or, Frontier Humor Comes to Town." *Studies in American Humor* 3, no. 4 (Winter 1984–85): 298–308.

Lawry, Jon S. "'Death in the Woods' and the Artist's Self in Sherwood Anderson." *PMLA* 74, no. 2 (June 1959): 306–11.

———. "The Arts of Winesburg and Bidwell, Ohio." *Twentieth Century Literature* 23, no. 1 (February 1977): 53–66.

Lindsay, Clarence. "Another Look at Community in *Winesburg, Ohio.*" *Midamerica* 20 (1993): 76–88.

———. "'I Belong in Little Towns': Sherwood Anderson's Small Town Postmodernism." *Midamerica* 26 (1999): 77–104.

Love, Glen A. "Horses or Men: Primitive and Pastoral Elements in Sherwood Anderson." In *Sherwood Anderson: Centennial Studies*, ed. Campbell and Modlin. 235–48.

Miller, Paul W. "Sherwood Anderson's Discovery of a Father." *Midamerica* 26 (1999): 113–20.

Miller, William V. "Earth-Mothers, Succubi, and Other Ectoplasmic Spirits: The Women in Sherwood Anderson's Short Stories." *Midamerica* 1 (1974): 64–81.

————. "Portraits of the Artist: Anderson's Fictional Storytellers." In *Sherwood Anderson: Dimensions of His Literary Art,* ed. Campbell and Modlin. 1–23.

————. "Texts, Subtexts and More Texts: Reconstructing the Narrator's Role in Sherwood Anderson's 'Death in the Woods.'" In *Exploring the Midwestern Literary Imagination,* ed. Marcia Noe. Troy, N.Y.: Whitston Publishers, 1993. 86–98.

Modlin, Charles E. "The Education of Sidney Adams: Anderson's 'Letters to Cynthia.'" *Sherwood Anderson Review* 25, no. 2 (2000), 5–11.

———— and Hilbert H. Campbell. "An Interview with Mrs. Sherwood Anderson." In *Sherwood Anderson: Centennial Studies,* ed. Campbell and Modlin. 67–77.

O'Neill, John. "Anderson Writ Large: 'Godliness' in *Winesburg, Ohio.*" *Twentieth Century Literature* 23, no. 1 (February 1977): 67–83.

Pfeiffer, William S. "*Mary Cochran*: Sherwood Anderson's Ten-Year Novel." *Studies in Bibliography* 31 (1978): 248–57.

Phillips, William L. "How Sherwood Anderson Wrote *Winesburg, Ohio.*" *American Literature* 23, no. 1 (March 1952): 7–30.

Rideout, Walter B. "Why Sherwood Anderson Employed Buck Fever." *Georgia Review* 13, no. 1 (Spring 1959): 76–85.

————. "The Sherwood Anderson Story." *Virginia Quarterly Review* 45, no. 4 (Autumn 1969): 537–40.

————. "Sherwood Anderson." In *Sixteen Modern American Authors: A Survey of Research and Criticism,* ed. Jackson R. Bryer. New York: Norton, 1973. 3–28.

————. "Talbott Whittingham and Anderson: A Passage to *Winesburg, Ohio.*" In *Sherwood Anderson: Dimensions of His Literary Art,* ed. Anderson. 41–60.

————. "'I Want to Know Why' as Biography and Fiction." *Midwestern Miscellany* 12 (1984): 7–14.

————. "'The Most Cultural Town in America': Sherwood Anderson and New Orleans." *Southern Review* 24, no. 1 (Winter 1988): 79–99.

————, ed. "Memories of Sherwood Anderson by His Brother Karl." *Winesburg Eagle* 16, no. 1 (Winter 1991): 1–14.

Rigsbee, Sally Adair. "The Feminine in *Winesburg, Ohio.*" *Studies in American Fiction* 9, no. 2 (Autumn 1981): 233–44.

Scafidel, J. R. "Sexuality in *Windy McPherson's Son.*" *Twentieth Century Literature* 23, no. 1 (February 1977): 94–101.

Scruggs, Charles. "The Reluctant Witness: What Jean Toomer Remembered from *Winesburg, Ohio.*" *Studies in American Fiction* 28, no. 1 (Spring 2000): 77–100.

Smith, Carl S. "*Windy McPherson's Son.*" *Chicago and the American Literary Imagination 1880–1920.* Chicago: University of Chicago Press, 1984. 78–87.

Spencer, Benjamin T. "Sherwood Anderson: American Mythopoeist." *American Literature* 41, no. 1 (March 1969): 126–44.

Stouck, David. "*Winesburg, Ohio* as a Dance of Death." *American Literature* 48, no. 1 (January 1977): 525–42.

————. "Anderson's Expressionist Art." In *New Essays on* Winesburg, Ohio, ed. Crowley. 27–51.

Sutton, William A. *The Revision of "Seeds."* Ball State University Studies. Muncie, Ind.: Ball State University Press, 1976.

Tanner, Tony. "Sherwood Anderson's Little Things." *The Reign of Wonder: Nativity and Reality in American Literature.* Cambridge: Cambridge University Press, 1965. 205–27.

Tanselle, G. Thomas. "The Case Western Reserve Edition of Sherwood Anderson: A Review Article." *Proof* 4 (1975): 183–209.

Turner, Darwin T. "An Intersection of Paths: Correspondence Between Jean Toomer and Sherwood Anderson." *College Language Association Journal* 17, no. 4 (June 1974): 455–67.

Whalen, Mark. "Dreams of Manhood: Narrative, Gender, and History in *Winesburg, Ohio*." *Studies in American Fiction* 30, no. 2 (Autumn 2002): 229–48.

White, Ray Lewis. "The Warmth of Desire: Sex in Anderson's Novels." In *Sherwood Anderson: Dimensions of His Literary Art,* ed. Anderson. 24–40.

Yingling, Thomas. "*Winesburg, Ohio* and the End of Collective Experience." In *New Essays on* Winesburg, Ohio, ed. Crowley. 99–128.

Index